CLEAN DESSERTS

Delicious No-Bake Vegan + Gluten-Free Cookies, Bars, Balls, and More

KARIELYN TILLMAN

www.thehealthyfamilyandhome.com

Skyhorse Publishing

Skyhorse Publishing books may be purchased in bulk at special discounts for sales promotion, corporate gifts, fund-raising, or educational purposes. Special editions can also be created to specifications. For details, contact the Special Sales Department, Skyhorse Publishing, 307 West 36th Street, 11th Floor, New York, NY 10018 or info@skyhorsepublishing.com.

Skyhorse® and Skyhorse Publishing® are registered trademarks of Skyhorse Publishing, Inc.®, a Delaware corporation.

Visit our website at www.skyhorsepublishing.com.

10 9 8 7 6 5 4 3

Library of Congress Cataloging-in-Publication Data is available on file.

Cover design by Karielyn Tillman
Cover photo credit by Karielyn Tillman

Print ISBN: 978-1-5107-4100-3
Ebook ISBN: 978-1-5107-4101-0

Printed in China

Dedication

To my two sons, Joshua + Augustin, who are the best kitchen
and photography helpers a mother could ask for;

My husband, Michael, whose hard work and daily sacrifices made
for our family have given me the opportunity to write this book;

And lastly to my Dad, who loved to eat the treats I made him and was
my most eager taste-tester. Sadly, he never got to see my book to completion.
I will forever miss making and bringing him treats.

JMJ | AMDG | BVM

Contents

Introduction

I know, you're probably thinking, "Great, another dessert cookbook." But this one is different, I promise!

If you've ever owned or flipped through a "no-bake" dessert cookbook, it's highly unlikely it was vegan *and* gluten-free; instead, it's likely that the recipes contained processed S.A.D. (Standard American Diet) ingredients like Cool Whip, Jell-O, M&M's, graham crackers, Oreo cookies, premade pie crusts, and other similar foods.

Additionally, recipes for vegan desserts sometimes use soy ingredients like tofu and soy milk, and other processed ingredients like white flour and white sugar and vegan "eggs," "cream cheese," "cottage cheese," "yogurt," "butter," etc.

And most gluten-free desserts use eggs, butter, cream cheese, cottage cheese, heavy cream, refined sugar, or complicated flour combinations, including stabilizers.

So, what do you do if you want to avoid processed ingredients while still enjoying vegan *and* gluten-free desserts? Well, I'm here to help with that!

This cookbook contains seventy-two vegan and gluten-free recipes all made with clean, real food ingredients. And even better—they're all no-bake!

I've included cookies, bars, balls, dessert squares, cheesecakes, tarts, ice cream, candy bars, and some well-known classic desserts. All vegan. All gluten-free. All clean ingredients.

If you've ever visited my website, *The Healthy Family and Home*, it's no secret that I absolutely love making clean desserts. Over the past seven years, I've created more than seven hundred recipes for my website, digital cookbook, and other published work, and it's apparent that my recipes are heavy on the dessert side! That's because I've never been able to do without my sweets.

Through the years, I've had to modify my diet for health reasons, but I was just not willing to give up dessert. How could I possibly never eat another brownie? Or ice cream in every flavor imaginable? Or cheesecake, cookies, and fudge?

I had to find a way to be able to enjoy desserts within the parameters of what I could eat. My mission was to make my recipes vegan (without butter, eggs, or cow milk), gluten-free (without grains or flour), refined sugar-free (naturally sweetened), and clean (without highly processed ingredients). This may seem like an impossible task, but it's exactly what I did. I learned which ingredients I could enjoy that were not detrimental to my health, and with this new list of clean ingredients I set out to "veganize" and remake traditional recipes, as well as create new ones, that were clean, gluten-free, and vegan. One dessert at a time.

What started as a way for me to continue enjoying desserts turned into a newfound passion. Seven years later, after sharing recipes on my website with readers all over the world, I continue to enjoy the challenge. Now, my passion and love for clean no-bake desserts are presented in this cookbook.

I hope you enjoy these unique recipes and will begin indulging in desserts without guilt. Don't ditch desserts—just change the way you make them, and feel good about what you eat!

What You Will Find in This Cookbook

This cookbook will change the way you feel about desserts. You may never want to make a traditional boxed dessert or S.A.D. dessert recipe again! And why would you, once you know how to make clean desserts?

What's Unique about These Desserts?

- **No-bake.** By spending less time in the kitchen, you can make several different recipes the same day or double batches of your favorites to stock in your freezer or refrigerator for a quick treat.
- **Clean, real food ingredients.** These recipes are made with real food with no highly processed ingredients, food colorings, preservatives, etc.
- **Vegan.** I do not use butter, dairy, or eggs.
- **Gluten-free.** I do not use grains or traditional flours; instead, these recipes use grain-free flours like almond flour and coconut flour.
- **Natural sweeteners.** All recipes are made with natural sweeteners and are just as sweet, if not sweeter, than desserts made with refined sugar. Natural sweeteners include medjool dates, maple syrup, and coconut sugar.
- **Easy substitutions.** Most of the nuts, nut butters, dried fruit, crusts, and add-ins are customizable and can be substituted. Get creative!
- **Easy clean-up.** Because there's no baking involved, there's less clean up!
- **Easy recipes.** Most of these easy-to-make recipes have prep times under 10 minutes.
- **Accessible equipment.** The only kitchen appliance you need to make these recipes is a basic food processor.
- **Core ingredient list.** I use a list of forty-eight easy-to-find core ingredients, and many can be bought in bulk and have a long shelf life.

Who Is This Book For?

- If you are tired of eating desserts made with S.A.D. (Standard American Diet) ingredients that make you feel heavy, lethargic, and regretful, this book is for you.
- If you are vegan and trying to avoid typical soy and processed ingredients like tofu, vegan "butter," or vegan "cream cheese"; or if you are someone just trying to avoid typical dairy ingredients like butter, eggs, and milk, this book is for you.
- If you are gluten-free and need recipes that are grain-free and do not contain white flour, wheat, gluten, or complicated flour combinations or stabilizers, this book is for you.
- If you are health conscious and tired of counting and eating empty calories and instead want to focus on nutrient-dense ingredients that nourish and fuel your body, this book is for you.
- If you're trying to eat clean with real foods and avoid highly processed ingredients like white sugar, food coloring, preservatives, artificial flavors, etc., this book is for you.
- If you're new in the kitchen, or even an experienced foodie, and don't like complicated recipes with long ingredient lists that require expensive equipment to make, this book is for you.

To make sure all your no-bake dessert needs and cravings are met, I've included six different types of recipes, reflected in these six chapters below:

Chapter 1 includes a variety of no-bake **cookies** that give you bite-sized, clean versions of cookies both familiar and new, like my "Chocolate Peanut Butter Oat Cookies," "Pecan Sandies Cookies," "Chocolate Pistachio Brownie Cookies,"and "Black Forest Thumbprint Cookies."

Chapter 2 features **bars** that will sustain you during the day. I use nutrient-dense ingredients like nuts, seeds, and nut butters to make treats like my "Crispy Chocolate Tahini Bars," "Cranberry + Cashew Chia Seed Bars," "Raspberry Pecan Fudge Bars," and "Blueberry Almond Granola Bars."

Chapter 3 gives you easy-to-make **balls**, so you can stock up on clean treats for when you need a quick energy boost. These are also perfect for portion control! Learn to make my "Lemon Ginger Sesame Seed Balls," "Chewy Oatmeal Cookie Balls," "Hazelnut Caramel Balls," and "Chocolate Chip Pecan + Oat Cookie Dough Balls."

Chapter 4 is my favorite—here, I make **dessert squares**! You'll find decadent and indulgent desserts that are great for entertaining or for special occasions, like my "Pomegranate + Caramel Brownie Squares," "Chocolate Pecan Pie Squares," "Peanut Butter + Chia Jam Swirl Squares," and "Triple Chocolate Almond Butter Squares."

Chapter 5 takes indulgent desserts one step further by showing you how to make show-stopping **cheesecakes, tarts, and ice cream**—all vegan and dairy-free with recipes like my "Kiwi + Coconut Cheesecake Squares," "Mango Chocolate Chip Cheesecake," "Blueberry Lemon Tarts with Almond Crust," and "Peanut Butter Brownie Ice Cream."

Finally, I can't send you away without the recipes in Chapter 6 for your clean dessert recipe arsenal—**candy bars and classics**! These are clean versions of all your favorite candy bars and classic desserts, like my "Snickers Bars," "Twix Bars," "Crispy Treat Squares," and "Pecan Pralines."

You can make all these recipes with nothing more than a food processor and a short list of easy-to-find ingredients. And don't forget, they are all vegan, gluten-free, dairy-free, refined sugar-free, and no-bake! It almost seems too good to be true—but it's not!

What Does "Clean Desserts" Even Mean?

Terms like "clean eating," "clean ingredients," and "clean desserts" can have different interpretations. But for the purpose of this cookbook, "clean" refers to the use of **real foods** that are closest to their natural state or minimally processed. It means eating as close to nature as possible. Clean ingredients are those that are unaltered, contain no additives or food colorings, are not difficult to pronounce, and not included in an ingredient list that's a paragraph long.

Here, clean ingredients are pecans, almonds, hazelnuts, hemp seeds, chia seeds, dates, coconut oil, etc., where the food item *is* the only ingredient. For example, the ingredient list for a bag of pecans is: pecans. The ingredient list for a bag of chia seeds is: chia seeds. Almond flour is almond flour, coconut oil is coconut oil, oats are oats, and so on.

On the contrary, the following are a few sample ingredient lists for store-bought S.A.D. foods that are typically used in no-bake desserts:

Kraft Jet-Puffed Marshmallows: Corn Syrup, Sugar, Dextrose, Modified Corn Starch, Water, Contains 2% or Less of Gelatin, Tetrasodium Pyrophosphate, Natural and Artificial Flavor, Blue 1

Pillsbury Refrigerated Pie Crust: Enriched Bleached Flour (Wheat Flour, Niacin, Ferrous Sulfate, Thiamin Mononitrate, Riboflavin, Folic Acid), Partially Hydrogenated Lard with BHA and BHT to Protect Flavor, Wheat Starch, Water, Contains 2% or Less of Salt, Rice Flour, Xanthan Gum, Potassium Sorbate (Preservative), Sodium Propionate (Preservative), Citric Acid, Yellow 5, Red 40

Colored Sprinkles: Sugar, Corn Starch, Vegetable Oil (Palm Kernel Oil and/or Palm Oil, Soy Lecithin, Dextrin, Confectioner's Glaze, Red 40 Lake, Natural and Artificial Flavor, Yellow 6 Lake, Carnauba Wax, Yellow 5 Lake, Blue 1 Lake, Red 3, Red 40

Jell-O, Strawberry Flavored: Sugar, Gelatin, Adipic Acid, Contains 2% or Less of Artificial Flavor, Disodium Phosphate, Sodium Citrate, Fumaric Acid, Red 40

The ingredient list for "Strawberry" flavored Jell-O, contains 0 percent of strawberries. Zero. It's artificially flavored, red food-colored sugar.

You will also notice in the previous four examples that none contained any "real" foods, or ingredients with any nutritional content whatsoever.

Here are a few more examples of store-bought S.A.D. foods often used in no-bake desserts—followed with a clean alternative:

Example 1:

Jell-O Chocolate Pudding Mix: Sugar, Modified Food Starch, Cocoa Processed with Alkali, Disodium Phosphate, Contains 2% or Less of Natural and Artificial Flavor, Salt, Tetrasodium Pyrophosphate, Monoglycerides, Diglycerides, Red 40, Yellow 5, Blue 1, Artificial Color, BHA (Preservative)

You don't have to give up chocolate pudding if you want to avoid an ingredient list like the one above. What if I gave you a recipe for a creamy chocolate pudding dessert that's made with real food ingredients?

Chocolate Avocado Pudding
(full recipe instructions can be found on my website at www.thehealthyfamilyandhome.com/creamy-chocolate-pudding/)

- 4 avocados
- ½ cup coconut sugar
- ¼ cup cacao powder
- 1 teaspoon pure vanilla extract
- 1 can full-fat coconut milk

My version has no preservatives, food colorings, artificial flavors, or white sugar, and is an excellent replacement for store-bought pudding. You won't even be able to taste the avocados!

Example 2:

Kraft Cool Whip: Water, Hydrogenated Vegetable Oil (Coconut and Palm Kernel Oils), High Fructose Corn Syrup, Corn Syrup, Skim Milk, Contains 2% or Less of Light Cream, Sodium Caseinate, Natural and Artificial Flavor, Xanthan and Guar Gums, Polysorbate 60, Sorbitan Monostearate, Sodium Polyphosphate, Beta Carotene (Color)

Some desserts just taste, and look, better with a dollop of whipped topping. But you don't have to pass it up because of the highly processed ingredient list above. Here is an excellent replacement for whipped topping that only has two ingredients:

Whipped Coconut Cream Topping
(full recipe instructions can be found on my website at www.thehealthyfamilyandhome.com/how-to-make-whipped-coconut-cream-topping/)

- 1 can full-fat coconut milk
- 2 tablespoons unrefined granular sweetener

You'll be amazed at how much this simple recipe tastes like store-bought Cool Whip, with even the same consistency, but without high fructose corn syrup, milk, stabilizers, and preservatives.

Example 3:

Kraft Caramels: Corn Syrup, Sugar, Skim Milk, Palm Oil, Whey (from Milk), Salt, Artificial Flavor, Soy Lecithin

Caramel is an indulgent ingredient that makes a dessert unique; some recipes are even created entirely around it. But you don't have to use store-bought caramel made with corn syrup, dairy, refined sugar, and artificial flavors when you can make your own with this easy recipe that takes less than 5 minutes to prepare:

Homemade Caramel Sauce

*(full recipe instructions can be found on my website at
www.thehealthyfamilyandhome.com/gluten-free-vegan-caramel-sauce/)*

- ½ cup almond butter
- ½ cup coconut oil
- ½ cup maple syrup
- ½ teaspoon vanilla
- ⅛ teaspoon sea salt

Now you can enjoy clean caramel treats using easy-to-find ingredients and without corn syrup, artificial flavor, and white sugar.

Now that you know what clean desserts are, let me explain what they are not.

Clean desserts are not low-calorie. They are not low-carb. They are not low-sugar. They are not low-fat. And they are not diet-friendly or conducive to weight-loss. Even though they are made with clean ingredients, they are still **desserts** that should be consumed in moderation. Even though these recipes contain natural sweeteners, they still contain sugar. And even though they contain healthy fats, they still register as fat.

Clean desserts are not exempt from fat, calories, carbs, or sugar. But they *are* exempt from highly processed ingredients, preservatives, food colorings, etc.

I've created these no-bake desserts to help you make a better choice whenever you crave an occasional treat—so you can indulge without guilt. I'm so excited for you to make and enjoy desserts you can finally feel good about eating!

What You Won't Find in This Cookbook

The following are ingredients and equipment you might typically find in a traditional no-bake dessert cookbook. They consist of a combination of premade and pre-packaged ingredients, like cookies, cakes, cereal, instant pudding mixes, candy bars, gelatin, pie fillings, maraschino cherries, boxed cheesecake mixes, Cool Whip, and Jell-O. Each of these singular ingredients can, in turn, have its own ingredient list the length of a short paragraph.

Ingredients

Marshmallows
Caramels
Colored Sprinkles
Jell-O
Cool-Whip
Packaged/Boxed Cake Mixes
Packaged/Boxed Instant Puddings
Packaged/Boxed Cereal
Store-Bought Pie Crusts
Store-Bought Pie Fillings
Graham Crackers
Vanilla Wafers
Oreo Cookies
Candy Bars
M&M's
Corn Syrup
Corn Starch
Food Colorings
Maraschino Cherries

Gelatin
Eggs
Butter
Margarine
White Flour
White Sugar
Powdered Sugar
Heavy Whipping Cream
Evaporated Milk
Condensed Milk
Cream Cheese
Sour Cream
Agave Nectar
Canola Oil
Xanthan Gum
Protein Powders
Soy Products (Soy Milk, Tofu)
Artificial Sweetener (Sucralose)
Artificial Sweetener (Aspartame)

Equipment

Microwave Oven
High-Speed Blender
Mixer
Ice Cream Maker
Dehydrator

And while boxed desserts are bad, don't assume that recipes for homemade desserts are any better. For example, a homemade no-bake cheesecake dessert may have an ingredient list that looks like this:

S.A.D. Homemade Cheesecake Ingredients

Crust: 1 package Oreo cookies, 1 stick butter, ½ cup colored sprinkles

Cheesecake: 20 oz cream cheese, 2 tablespoons heavy whipping cream, ¼ cup white sugar, ½ cup vanilla cake mix, ¼ cup colored sprinkles, 10 crushed Oreo cookies

Filling: 4 ounces cream cheese, 1½ cups heavy whipping cream, 1 cup powdered sugar, 2 tablespoons cocoa powder

Topping: ¾ cup heavy whipping cream, ½ cup powdered sugar, 5 crushed Oreo cookies, 1 tablespoons colored sprinkles

This is a real recipe that includes an entire box of Oreo cookies, an entire stick of butter, a total of 1¾ cups of refined sugar, a boxed cake mix, 4 packages of cream cheese, and over 2 cups of heavy whipping cream—all of these processed ingredients to make only 8 to 10 slices.

You probably can't imagine making a no-bake cheesecake without using at least one or more of these ingredients. Believe me, I've eaten my share of S.A.D. desserts back in the day, but now I know that you don't have to make or eat these types of treats anymore. For example, let's look at the recipe for a creamy no-bake cheesecake dessert like my "Kiwi + Coconut Cheesecake Squares" (full recipe on pg. 157):

Kiwi + Coconut Cheesecake Squares Ingredients

Crust: 2 cups pecans, 1 cup medjool dates, ½ cup unsweetened shredded coconut, 2 tablespoons coconut oil, 1 teaspoon vanilla extract, and ⅛ teaspoon sea salt

Cheesecake: 3 cups cashews, ½ cup maple syrup, 4 kiwi, ¼ cup lemon juice, ¼ cup coconut oil, ⅛ teaspoon sea salt

Topping: ½ cup unsweetened shredded coconut, 2–3 sliced kiwi

Here's a side-by-side comparison list of the ingredients from these two recipes:

S.A.D. INGREDIENTS	CLEAN INGREDIENTS
Oreo cookies	Pecans
Butter	Coconut Oil
Colored Sprinkles	Unsweetened Shredded Coconut
Cream Cheese	Cashews
Heavy Whipping Cream	Lemon Juice
White Sugar	Maple Syrup
Boxed Vanilla Cake Mix	Kiwi
Powdered Sugar	Medjool Dates

In all fairness, both are high in carbs, high in fat, and high in sugar content. But there is nothing in the list on the left with any significant nutritional value, whereas the ingredients on the right are real, unprocessed, and nutrient-dense.

The ingredients I use, and don't use, are what make my cookbook different from traditional no-bake dessert cookbooks. I hope you will keep reaching for it over and over again whenever you want to make a dessert!

What to Expect from Clean No-Bake Desserts

If you are new to no-bake desserts or even clean desserts, here's what you can expect. While there's not too much that can go wrong when making these recipes since there is no baking involved, here are some tips to help ensure that you will be successful.

Inactive Time: Although there is no baking time in no-bake desserts, there will be inactive time—time when there is no hands-on attention needed. This is when the desserts will be placed in either the freezer or refrigerator to set and firm before they are ready to enjoy. The prep time on most of the recipes is typically 10 minutes or less, but the inactive time can be considerably longer, even overnight for a few recipes.

This shouldn't be a problem if you plan in advance. You'll need to remember to make your desserts *before* you get a sweet craving, because you won't be able to eat them right away. If you are planning to serve guests, make sure to consider the inactive time, too. Check the total preparation time (prep + inactive) before starting a recipe to ensure you have allotted enough time, and you'll be fine!

Binders: Because my clean desserts do not contain typical binding ingredients like corn syrup, eggs, flour, or butter, they rely on just a few trusty ingredients to hold everything together. Without these ingredients, the desserts would literally fall apart, so you'll see them used often throughout the cookbook.

- **Dates**: Dates are an excellent binder in the ball, bar, and crust recipes. They are also a perfect natural sweetener that is also nutrient-dense.
- **Coconut Oil:** When coconut oil is in a liquid state (usually over 75 degrees), it mixes into your ingredients with ease. But once it hardens (when frozen or refrigerated), it turns into a solid and perfectly holds everything together in the ball, bar, and crust recipes.

Storage + Traveling: The recipes that do not contain coconut oil should hold up enough to be packed in a lunchbox or left out on the countertop. But those that contain coconut oil will not hold up at room temperature like traditional recipes, because they will get soft, lose their shape, or get messy due to the coconut oil changing consistency at room temperature. This isn't a problem if you keep your desserts in the freezer or refrigerator until ready to serve, to maintain their shape and consistency. You wouldn't want to pack a treat in a lunch bag or bring a tray of bars to a party, only to have them melted when you arrive. Keep this in mind if you're preparing something that you won't be enjoying at home.

Ingredients

Y ou won't need hard-to-find ingredients or ones you've never even heard of in this cookbook. All the ingredients I use can be found at major grocery stores, including Target and Whole Foods, as well as online at Vitacost, Terrasoul, Thrive Market, and Amazon.

Below, I've listed 48 core ingredients that will be featured in these recipes. Feel free to experiment by mixing and matching your favorite ingredients or make substitutions for anything you don't have on hand. Since most of these have a long shelf life, you can purchase in bulk to save money. This makes it easy to always keep your pantry stocked with clean ingredients.

Note: It's best to purchase organic and/or non-GMO ingredients whenever possible.

Nuts
Almonds
Cashews
Hazelnuts
Peanuts
Pecans
Pistachios
Walnuts

Nut Butters
Almond Butter
Cashew Butter
Peanut Butter
Tahini

Seeds
Chia Seeds
Hemp Seeds
Sesame Seeds
Sunflower Seeds

Natural Sweeteners
Coconut Sugar
Maple Syrup
Medjool Dates

Flours
Almond Flour
Coconut Flour

Spices
Cacao Powder
Cinnamon
Ginger
Pumpkin Spice
Sea Salt
Vanilla Extract

Oils
Coconut Oil

Dried Fruit

Apricots
Bananas
Blueberries
Cranberries
Raspberries
Strawberries

Fresh Fruit

Avocado
Bananas
Dark Sweet Cherries
Kiwi
Lemons
Mango
Pomegranate

Other Add-Ins

Coconut Flakes
Quick Rolled Oats
Unsweetened Shredded Coconut

Miscellaneous

Brown Rice Crisps Cereal
Coconut Milk
Garbanzo Beans (Chickpeas)
Pumpkin Puree
Semi-Sweet Mini Chocolate Chips

Nuts

(almonds, cashews, hazelnuts, peanuts, pecans, pistachios, walnuts)

Nuts are pretty much interchangeable with each other except for the ones with distinct flavors, like hazelnuts, peanuts, and pistachios.

Almond, Cashews, Pecans, Walnuts: For these, I used raw and unsalted nuts. Each of these are great to substitute with another nut, especially if you don't like the flavor of a particular one or don't have it on hand, with the exception of cashews, noted below.

Cashews: Cashews are a neutrally flavored nut that are interchangeable with other nuts. However, one exception is that cashews cannot be substituted when they are used in the cheesecake, tart, and ice cream recipes. The cashews here are what give the recipe its creaminess and neutral flavor, which other nuts cannot provide. In these recipes, you will need to soak the cashews for at least one hour, and then drain and rinse before using. Additionally, it's also important to use raw cashews that are not roasted or salted because they would affect the flavor of the dessert.

Peanuts, Pistachios: For these nuts, I used roasted and salted. If you use unsalted nuts, you may want to adjust the salt in the recipe slightly.

Nut Butters

(almond butter, cashew butter, peanut butter, tahini)

Some neutral nut butters, like cashew and almond butter, can be substituted interchangeably, but peanut butter, for example, will affect the flavor of the recipe.

Almond Butter, Cashew Butter, Peanut Butter: Make sure you check the ingredients for added salt, sugar, and oil, and make adjustments in the recipe for flavor and consistency as needed. For example, the brand of nut butter you use could affect the consistency of a recipe. If your nut butter is extra thick, you may need to add extra liquid. Or if your nut butter is a little runny, you may need to add extra almond flour or coconut flour to firm the mixture. Start with the recommended amount of nut butter in the recipe and adjust additional liquid or flour in small amounts as needed. For the recipes in this cookbook, I used creamy natural nut butters.

Tahini (Ground Sesame Seeds): Tahini is made from ground sesame seeds and has a unique flavor that you will either love or hate. If you don't like the taste of tahini, substitute it with a neutral nut butter like almond or cashew. Tahini can also have added salt or oil, so make sure you check your label and make adjustments in the recipe as needed for flavor and consistency. I used unhulled ground tahini for the recipes that required tahini.

A great way to save money on nut butters is to make your own. Nut butters, and even tahini, can be easily made with a food processor with a little time and patience. Simply add the nuts to your food processor and process. It will go through several stages—nuts to nut flour, and finally nut flour to nut butter. It takes about 5 to 7 minutes, and you will need to stop and scrape down the sides a couple of times to help it along. This is a great way to enjoy 100 percent pure nut butter with nothing else added.

You can find an easy recipe for Homemade Peanut Butter on my website at www.thehealthyfamilyandhome.com/how-to-make-homemade-peanut-butter/. Get creative and add a little coconut oil, cinnamon, maple syrup, vanilla, or cacao powder to make delicious flavored nut butters!

Seeds
(chia seeds, hemp seeds, sesame seeds, sunflower seeds)

Nutrient-dense seeds were added to these recipes primarily for extra nutrition, and for the crunchy texture they provide. They can be omitted or substituted with another seed—or even one of your favorite nuts.

Chia seeds come in a couple of different varieties, white or black, and you can use either one. Raw and unsalted sunflower seeds, unhulled sesame seeds, and shelled hemp seeds were used in these recipes, but feel free to use whatever you have on hand.

You can buy seeds in the bulk section of grocery stores like Whole Foods and store them in an air-tight glass mason jar to maintain freshness.

Natural Sweeteners
(coconut sugar, maple syrup, medjool dates)

Coconut Sugar: This is an excellent replacement for refined white sugar because it's minimally processed and unrefined. I used it in recipes that require a granular sweetener.

Maple Syrup: Make sure you use pure maple syrup and not store-bought maple-flavored pancake syrup—they are not the same. The ingredient list for the latter is: *Corn Syrup, High Fructose Corn Syrup, Water, Contains 2% or Less of: Cellulose Gum, Salt, Sorbic Acid (Preservative), Sodium Benzoate (Preservative), Honey, Sodium Citrate, Caramel Color, Natural Flavors and Artificial Flavors*. The ingredient list for pure maple syrup is: *Maple Syrup*.

Dates: I *love* using dates as a natural sweetener. I use medjool dates, which are larger than another common variety, deglet noor dates. Dates are a great alternative to refined white sugar, and they contain vitamins, minerals, fiber, and antioxidants. These bite-sized treats are delicious by themselves and great for a quick boost of energy—simply slice one in half and fill it with your favorite nut butter!

When a recipe calls for 1 cup of medjool dates, it usually equals about 10 pitted dates. Always measure to be sure because the dates will vary in size, especially if you use a variety other than medjool. And, before you add dates to your food processor, make sure they are pitted first by slicing them in half and removing the pits.

Flours
(almond flour, coconut flour)

The two flours I used in this cookbook, almond flour and coconut flour, are both gluten-free and wheat-free. They cannot be used interchangeably because they have different consistencies.

Almond Flour: Almond flour is typically used as a clean substitution for white, wheat, and gluten flours. There are different varieties of almond flours such as almond meal (coarse, with the skin) and almond flour (lighter and fluffier, blanched without the skin). I used Bob's Red Mill Super Fine Almond Flour for all recipes that required almond flour.

Coconut Flour: Coconut flour is a very dense flour and primarily used in these recipes to thicken and absorb liquids. For example, depending on the type of nut butter used in a recipe, you may need to add an extra tablespoon or two of coconut flour to thicken up a mixture, but only use as needed. Using too much coconut flour will result in an overly dry mixture.

Spices
(cacao powder, cinnamon, ginger, pumpkin spice, sea salt, vanilla extract)

You may already have these basic staples in your pantry—ground cinnamon, ground ginger, and ground pumpkin spice. Feel free to adjust the measurement amount of any of these spices according to your taste preference.

Cacao Powder: This is the raw, unprocessed version of cocoa powder. You can substitute cacao powder with cocoa powder in any of the recipes.

Sea Salt: I primarily use Himalayan pink salt because it is unrefined, unprocessed and raw, but feel free to use sea salt or whatever type of salt you have on hand.

Vanilla Extract: Make sure the vanilla extract you use is "pure" vanilla extract and not artificially flavored.

Oils

(coconut oil)

If you do a Google search on whether coconut oil is good or bad for you, you will find both pros and cons. I personally believe that coconut oil is a healthier fat in comparison to canola oil or vegetable oil, when used in moderation. It's an essential ingredient in many of these no-bake recipes for its binding properties.

There are two types of coconut oil—unrefined and refined. Unrefined coconut oil will smell and taste like coconut, while refined coconut oil has no coconut smell or taste. They both perform the same function in these recipes, so which version you choose to use is a matter of personal preference. Since I use coconut oil primarily for binding purposes and not flavor, my preference is to use refined so that the coconut flavor doesn't overpower the other flavors.

Dried Fruit

(apricots, bananas, blueberries, cranberries, raspberries, strawberries)

Dried fruits are used to impart a fruity flavor since using fresh fruit would make the dessert soggy, especially in bar, cookie, and ball recipes. Dried fruit is great not only because it lends a strong fruit flavor to the recipe, but also because it provides a little crunch.

Try to find freeze-dried fruit with no added sugar, where the only ingredient is the fruit itself.

Fresh Fruit

(avocados, bananas, dark sweet cherries, kiwi, lemons, mango, pomegranate)

Most of the fresh fruit used in these recipes can be either fresh or frozen, except for avocado and pomegranate.

Bananas: The bananas used in the "nice" cream recipe are best when they are ripe as they are used as the sweetener. Wait until your bananas start spotting before you put them in the freezer in preparation to make the recipe.

Dark Sweet Cherries: I used frozen, pitted, dark sweet cherries. If you use fresh cherries, make sure they are pitted before adding them to your food processor. You can use any variety of cherries, just stay away from the bright red maraschino cherries that come in a glass jar and contain food coloring and preservatives.

Kiwi: If kiwi isn't in season, you can substitute it with another tropical fruit that would pair well with coconut, such as pineapples, mango, or bananas.

Lemons: Freshly squeezed lemons, which are not pasteurized, will give you a more intense lemon flavor and more nutrients than store-bought lemon juice. However, you can also use the latter.

Mango: If mango isn't in season, you can use frozen cubed mango.

Other Add-Ins
(coconut flakes, oats, shredded coconut)

These add-ins are used as both a main ingredient and as a garnish in some recipes. If you don't like coconut and it's not a main ingredient in a recipe, you can omit it.

Coconut Flakes: These large, flaked coconut pieces are different from shredded coconut. You can substitute coconut flakes with unsweetened shredded coconut in the same amount.

Oats: I use Bob's Red Mill Gluten-Free Quick Rolled Oats primarily because they are organic and gluten-free. There are different varieties of oats, such as rolled oats and steel-cut oats, which will not perform the same function as quick rolled oats in these recipes.

Unsweetened Shredded Coconut: Unsweetened shredded coconut does not have any added sweetener. If you use sweetened shredded coconut, you may need to adjust the amount of sweetener in the recipe.

Miscellaneous Ingredients
(brown rice crisps cereal, semi-sweet mini chocolate chips, coconut milk, garbanzo beans [chickpeas], pumpkin puree)

There are a few minimally processed ingredients that can't theoretically be considered "real food," but they are still cleaner versions of traditional store-bought brands. Try to find brands that have a short ingredient list with clean ingredients, and try to buy organic, if possible. Below, I've listed a few examples of clean products I use in comparison to more processed alternatives.

Brown Rice Cereal: I use the Whole Foods brand of brown rice cereal because it is organic, gluten-free, and only contains three clean ingredients.

- **Whole Foods 365 Organic Brown Rice Crisps Cereal Ingredients:** Organic Whole Grain Brown Rice, Organic Cane Sugar, Sea Salt
- **Kellogg's Rice Krispies Cereal Ingredients:** Rice, Sugar, Salt, Malt Flavoring, Iron, Ascorbic Acid (Vitamin C), Alpha Tocopherol Acetate (Vitamin E), Niacinamide, Vitamin A Palmitate, Pyridoxine Hydrochloride (Vitamin B6), Riboflavin (Vitamin B2), Thiamin Hydrochloride (Vitamin B1), Folic Acid, Vitamin B12 and Vitamin D

Semi-Sweet Mini Chocolate Chips: I use the Enjoy Life brand of chocolate chips because it only contains three ingredients, is Non-GMO Project Verified, and is allergy-free with no dairy, soy, or artificial flavors.

- **Enjoy Life Semi-Sweet Chocolate Chip Ingredients:** Cane Sugar, Unsweetened Chocolate, Cocoa Butter
- **Nestlé's Chocolate Chips:** Semi-Sweet Chocolate (Sugar, Chocolate, Cocoa Butter, Milkfat, Soy Lecithin, Natural Flavors)

Coconut Milk (Full-Fat, Canned): I use the Native Forest brand of coconut milk because it is organic, contains three ingredients, and comes in a BPA-free lined can.

- **Native Forest Organic Coconut Milk Classic:** Organic Coconut Milk, Purified Water, Organic Guar Gum
- **Goya Coconut Milk**: Coconut Extract, Water, Citric Acid, Sodium Metabisulfite

Garbanzo Beans (Chickpeas): I like the Eden Organic brand because it is organic, contains three ingredients, has no added salt, and comes in a BPA-free lined can.
- **Eden Organic Garbanzo Beans:** Organic Garbanzo Beans, Water, Kombu Seaweed

- **Bush's Garbanzo Chick Peas:** Prepared Chick Peas, Water, Salt, Calcium Chloride, Disodium EDTA

Pumpkin Puree: Even though there are options for a 100 percent pure pumpkin puree, I like to use the Farmer's Market brand—it's organic and comes in a BPA-free lined can.

- **Farmer's Market Organic Pumpkin Puree:** Certified Organic Pumpkin
- **Libby's 100% Pure Pumpkin:** Pumpkin

Kitchen Tools

You'll be glad to know that you'll only need one kitchen appliance to make the recipes here—a simple food processor. If you don't have a food processor, it's not necessary to purchase an expensive one. There are many different brands and models to choose from in all price ranges. Since I use my food processor almost every day, I use a larger, heavy-duty KitchenAid 11-Cup Food Processor and was used to make the recipes in this cookbook.

Below is a list of the kitchen tools needed:

Food Processor
Parchment Paper
8 × 8 Baking Dish
9 × 5 Loaf Pan
Cookie Sheet
Air-Tight BPA-Free Containers
Silicone or Paper Muffin Cups (Standard Size + Mini)
1½-Inch Cookie Scoop (Optional)
12-Cavity Mini-Cheesecake Pan (Optional)
4-Inch Tart Dishes (Optional)
6-Inch Springform Cheesecake Pan (Optional)

Food Processor: A food processor is great for breaking down dates, nuts, and seeds, as well as combining everything together uniformly. One of my goals when writing this cookbook was to make these recipes accessible to everyone by using only one common kitchen appliance—a food processor. I didn't want to alienate readers by relying on expensive equipment like a high-speed blender, a mixer, microwave, or even an ice cream maker. However, if you do have a high-speed blender, feel free to use it because you will get optimal results, especially with the cheesecake, tart, and ice cream recipes, as it will provide an ultra-smooth texture. If you're using a food processor for these particular recipes, you can still get good results with a little prep time: you'll need to take an extra step to soak the cashews in advance to soften them for easy blending.

Parchment Paper: If you don't already use parchment paper, I recommend you purchase this key item. Parchment paper is a non-toxic, disposable, non-stick paper that makes removing cookies, dates, bars, etc., easy and keeps them from sticking to your cookie sheet or baking dish. And clean-up is much easier, too! I prefer to use unbleached parchment paper, but regular is fine, too.

8 × 8 Baking Dish / 9 × 5 Loaf Pan / Cookie Sheet: You will need each of these to make the desserts here. The 8 × 8 baking dish is used for bars and squares; the 9 × 5 loaf pan is used for bars, squares, candy bars, fudge, and ice cream; and the cookie sheet is used for cookies, balls, and candies. For the baking dishes, you can use either a metal or glass variety. Remember, you won't actually be baking in any of them.

Air-Tight BPA-Free Containers: These containers are great to keep your goodies fresh in the freezer or refrigerator. I have eliminated plastic containers from my kitchen and prefer to use glass and/or BPA-free containers. Make sure the containers you use are air-tight to maintain freshness for as long as possible and to prevent freezer burn.

Silicone or Paper Muffin Cups: I love my faithful set of standard-size muffin cups. I've used the same set for almost eight years—and they're still going strong. They are reusable and easy to clean, and you never have to worry about running out like you would with paper muffin cups. They are especially great to have on hand to use for mini, bite-size, or individual desserts—even chocolate candy! If you don't have a springform cheesecake pan or a tart pan, use these silicone muffin cups instead by simply dividing the mixture equally among the muffin cups.

Cookie Scoop (Optional): This is a fun cooking tool I like to use to scoop the mixture for cookies and balls because it keeps the measurements consistent. If you don't have one, you can always use a spoon. Cookie scoops come in different sizes, and I use the 1½-inch scoop for the recipes here, which is equivalent to 1 tablespoon.

12-Cavity Mini Cheesecake Pan (Optional): This is another fun cooking tool that makes such a difference in the presentation of your desserts by giving them a professional appearance. If you don't have one, you can use a standard-size muffin cup to make individual servings.

4-inch Tart Pan / Dish (Optional): A tart pan gives your tarts a professional-looking wavy crust border. I like to use two different varieties. The first is a 4-inch tart pan with removable bottom disks that allow the crust to be easily removed. You can then slice and serve the tart separate from the tart pan. My other favorite variety is a 4-inch ramekin tart dish, which the actual tart is served in. If you don't have either, you can always make the dessert into individual servings by using standard-size muffin cups.

6-inch Springform Cheesecake Pan (Optional): This larger cheesecake pan is great for when you make a dessert for a larger crowd, or if you want to serve a standard-size serving of cheesecake. Just like the tart dish, it comes with a removable bottom disk, which allows the crust to be easily removed. I use the 6-inch pan for the recipes here, but note that they also come in different sizes.

1
cookies

CHOCOLATE PEANUT BUTTER OAT COOKIES

Yields: 16 small cookies | **Prep Time:** 10 minutes | **Inactive Time:** 30 minutes

INGREDIENTS

For the cookies:
½ cup peanut butter
½ cup coconut oil
½ cup maple syrup
¼ cup cacao powder
¼ teaspoon vanilla extract

For the add-in:
2 cups gluten-free quick rolled oats

DIRECTIONS

1. Prepare a cookie sheet lined with parchment paper. Set aside.

2. Add all ingredients for the cookies to a medium-sized bowl and stir until everything is well combined and smooth.

3. Add the oats and stir until they are evenly distributed.

4. Take one spoonful of mixture at a time and drop it onto the prepared cookie sheet.

5. Transfer the cookie sheet to the freezer for approximately 30 minutes, or until the cookies are firm.

6. Store in an air-tight container in the freezer or refrigerator until ready to serve, because the cookies will get soft if left out at room temperature.

BLACK FOREST THUMBPRINT COOKIES

Yields: 16 small cookies | **Prep Time:** 15 minutes | **Inactive Time:** 30 minutes

INGREDIENTS

For the cookies:
2½ cups almond flour
½ cup cashew butter
¼ cup coconut flour
¼ cup coconut oil
⅓ cup maple syrup
½ teaspoon vanilla extract
⅛ teaspoon sea salt

For the cherry filling:
1 cup dark sweet cherries, pitted
2 large medjool dates, pitted
1 tablespoon chia seeds

For the chocolate drizzle:
¼ cup semi-sweet mini chocolate chips
½ teaspoon coconut oil

DIRECTIONS

Prepare the cookies:

1. Prepare a cookie sheet lined with parchment paper. Set aside.

2. Add all ingredients for the cookies to a medium-sized bowl and stir until everything is well combined.

3. Take one spoonful of the mixture at a time, squeeze it tightly in your fist to make it compact, then gently roll it between the palms of your hands into a ball shape. Depending on the consistency of the cashew butter, you may need to add extra coconut flour until the mixture is firm enough to roll into a ball shape. Add 1 teaspoon at a time until it firms, but only as needed.

4. Flatten the ball between the palms of your hands into a round cookie shape about 2 inches in diameter. Place the cookies onto the prepared cookie sheet.

5. When you have finished preparing all the cookies, press down in the center of

(continued on next page)

each cookie with your thumb to form a "thumbprint," or a space deep enough to hold the cherry filling. Set aside.

Prepare the cherry filling:

1. Add all ingredients for the cherry filling to a food processor and process until the cherries and dates are broken down into small pieces. Set aside.

2. Take a small spoonful of the cherry filling and fill in the center of each cookie.

Prepare the chocolate drizzle:

1. Add all ingredients for the chocolate drizzle to a small saucepan and melt on lowest heat, stirring until it is completely melted and smooth, taking care to not let it burn. Set aside.

2. Using a spoon, drizzle the melted chocolate over the top of each cookie.

Assembly:

1. Transfer the cookie sheet to the freezer for approximately 30 minutes, or until the cookies are firm.

2. Store in an air-tight container in the freezer or refrigerator until ready to serve, because the cookies will get soft if left out at room temperature.

CHOCOLATE HAZELNUT COOKIES

Yields: 8 small cookies | **Prep Time:** 10 minutes | **Inactive Time:** 30 minutes

INGREDIENTS

For the cookies:
⅔ cup hazelnuts
6 tablespoons almond flour
3 tablespoons maple syrup
2 tablespoons cacao powder
1 teaspoon vanilla extract
⅛ teaspoon sea salt

For the hazelnut topping:
¼ cup hazelnuts, chopped

For the chocolate coating:
1 cup semi-sweet mini chocolate chips
1 tablespoon coconut oil

DIRECTIONS

Prepare the hazelnut topping:

1. Place the hazelnuts on a flat surface, like a countertop, and using the flat side of a butter knife, crush the hazelnuts into tiny pieces, as small as possible. Set aside.

Prepare the cookies:

1. Prepare a cookie sheet lined with parchment paper. Set aside.

2. Add all ingredients for the cookies to a food processor and process until the hazelnuts are broken down into small pieces and everything is well combined, taking care to not over process.

3. Take one spoonful of the mixture at a time, squeeze it tightly in your fist to make it compact, then flatten it between the palms of your hands into a round cookie shape about 2 inches in diameter.

4. Place the chopped hazelnuts on a flat surface, like a countertop. Take one cookie at a time and press the top of each cookie down into the chopped

(continued on next page)

hazelnuts, doing this on both sides. Gently pat the hazelnuts down into the cookie so they don't fall off.

5. Place the cookies onto the prepared cookie sheet. Transfer the cookie sheet to the freezer for the cookies to firm while you prepare the chocolate coating.

Prepare the chocolate coating:

1. Add all ingredients for the chocolate coating to a small saucepan and stir on lowest heat, stirring until it is completely melted and smooth, taking care to not let it burn.

2. Remove the cookie sheet from the freezer and dip each cookie into the chocolate coating until the cookie is completely covered on all sides. Use a fork to flip them over and to allow the excess chocolate to drip off.

Assembly:

1. 1. Place the cookies back onto the cookie sheet. Return the cookie sheet to the freezer for approximately 30 minutes, or until the chocolate hardens.

2. Store in an air-tight container in the freezer or refrigerator until they are ready to serve, because the cookies will get soft if left out at room temperature.

tip: Instead of dipping the entire cookie into the chocolate coating, you can also drizzle the chocolate coating over the top of the cookies to reveal the chopped hazelnuts for a more dramatic appearance!

PEANUT BUTTER + DATE HEMP SEED COOKIES

Yields: 14 small cookies | **Prep Time:** 10 minutes | **Inactive Time:** 30 minutes

INGREDIENTS

For the cookies:
1 cup peanut butter
1 cup medjool dates, pitted
½ cup hemp seeds
1 tablespoon coconut flour
1 teaspoon vanilla extract
¼ teaspoon sea salt
⅛ teaspoon ground cinnamon

DIRECTIONS

1. Prepare a cookie sheet lined with parchment paper. Set aside.

2. Add all ingredients to a food processor and process until the dates are broken down into small pieces and everything is well combined, taking care to not over process.

3. Take one spoonful of the mixture at a time and roll it between the palms of your hands into a ball shape.

4. Flatten the ball between the palms of your hands into a round cookie shape about 2 inches in diameter. Place the cookies onto the prepared cookie sheet.

5. Using a fork, make a "criss-cross" fork indention into the top of each cookie.

6. Transfer the cookie sheet to the freezer for approximately 30 minutes, or until the cookies are firm.

7. Store in an air-tight container in the freezer or refrigerator until they are ready to serve, because the cookies will get soft if left out at room temperature.

LEMON BLUEBERRY COOKIES

Yields: 12 small cookies | **Prep Time:** 10 minutes | **Inactive Time:** 30 minutes

INGREDIENTS

For the cookies:
1½ cups almond flour
¼ cup lemon juice
¼ cup maple syrup
⅓ cup coconut flour
½ teaspoon vanilla extract
⅛ teaspoon sea salt

For the add-in:
1 cup freeze-dried blueberries

tip: A quicker option is to add all the blueberries directly into the cookie mixture and gently stir in by hand. The blueberries will "bleed" into the cookie mixture, giving the cookies a "purplish" color, but they will taste the same.

DIRECTIONS

1. Prepare a cookie sheet lined with parchment paper. Set aside.

2. Add all ingredients for the cookies to a food processor and process until everything is well combined.

3. Take one spoonful of the mixture at a time, and place in the center of one hand. With your other hand, gently press in 6 to 7 dried blueberries into the cookie mixture, making sure they are evenly distributed. This step will retain the original color of the cookie mixture by keeping the blueberries from "bleeding."

4. Flatten the cookie mixture between the palms of your hands into a round cookie shape about 2 inches in diameter. Place the cookies onto the prepared cookie sheet.

5. Transfer the cookie sheet to the freezer for approximately 30 minutes, or until the cookies are firm.

6. Store in an air-tight container in the freezer or refrigerator until ready to serve, because the cookies will get soft if left out at room temperature.

CHOCOLATE PISTACHIO BROWNIE COOKIES

Yields: 10 small cookies | **Prep Time:** 10 minutes | **Inactive Time:** 30 minutes

INGREDIENTS

For the cookies:
1 cup pistachios
1 cup medjool dates, pitted
2 tablespoons cacao powder
1 tablespoon water
1 teaspoon vanilla extract
⅛ teaspoon sea salt

For the pistachio topping:
¼ cup pistachios, chopped

DIRECTIONS

Prepare the pistachio topping:

1. Place the pistachios on a flat surface, like a countertop, and, using the flat side of a butter knife, crush the pistachios into tiny pieces, as small as possible. Set aside.

Prepare the cookies:

1. Prepare a cookie sheet lined with parchment paper. Set aside.

2. Add all ingredients for the cookies to a food processor and process until the pistachios and dates are broken down into small pieces and everything is well combined, taking care to not over process.

3. Take one spoonful of the mixture at a time, squeeze it tightly in your fist to make it compact, then gently roll it between the palms of your hands into a ball shape.

4. Flatten the ball between the palms of your hands into a round cookie shape about 2 inches in diameter.

5. Place the chopped pistachios on a flat surface, like a countertop. Take one cookie at a time and press the top of each cookie down into the chopped pistachios.

6. Gently pat the pistachios down into the cookie so they don't fall off. Place the cookies onto the prepared cookie sheet.

7. Transfer the cookie sheet to the freezer for approximately 30 minutes, or until the cookies are firm.

8. Store in an air-tight container in the freezer or refrigerator until ready to serve, because the cookies will get soft if left out at room temperature.

CARAMEL PECAN OAT COOKIES

INGREDIENTS

For the caramel:
½ cup almond butter
½ cup coconut oil
½ cup maple syrup
½ teaspoon vanilla extract
⅛ teaspoon sea salt

For the cookies:
2 cups gluten-free quick rolled oats
½ cup pecans, chopped
½ cup semi-sweet mini chocolate chips

DIRECTIONS

Prepare the caramel:

1. Add all ingredients for the caramel to a medium-sized bowl and stir until everything is well combined and smooth. Set aside.

Prepare the cookies:

1. Prepare a cookie sheet lined with parchment paper. Set aside.

2. Add the ingredients for the cookies to the bowl of caramel and stir until well combined and evenly distributed.

3. Take one spoonful of the mixture at a time and drop it onto the prepared cookie sheet.

4. Transfer the cookie sheet to the freezer for approximately 30 minutes, or until the cookies are firm.

5. Store in an air-tight container in the freezer or refrigerator until ready to serve, because the cookies will get soft if left out at room temperature.

DRIED APRICOT + CHOCOLATE CHIP COOKIES

Yields: 14 small cookies | **Prep Time:** 10 minutes | **Inactive Time:** 30 minutes

INGREDIENTS

For the cookies:
1 cup almond flour
½ cup cashew butter
¼ cup maple syrup
½ cup sun-dried apricots
½ teaspoon vanilla extract
⅛ teaspoon sea salt

For the add-in:
½ cup semi-sweet mini chocolate chips

DIRECTIONS

1. Prepare a cookie sheet lined with parchment paper. Set aside.

2. Add all ingredients for the cookies to a food processor and process until the apricots are broken down into small pieces and everything is well combined, taking care to not over process. Depending on the consistency of the cashew butter, you may need to add extra coconut flour until the mixture has a "cookie dough" texture. Add 1 teaspoon at a time until it firms, but only as needed.

3. Add the chocolate chip add-in to the food processor and stir in by hand until they are evenly distributed.

4. Using a 1½-inch cookie scoop or a regular spoon, take one scoop of the mixture at a time and place it onto the prepared cookie sheet. You can either leave them in a fun "cookie scoop" shape as shown in the photo or flatten them into a traditional round cookie shape about 2 inches in diameter.

5. Transfer the cookie sheet to the freezer for approximately 30 minutes, or until the cookies are firm.

6. Store in an air-tight container in the freezer or refrigerator until ready to serve, because the cookies will get soft if left out at room temperature.

tip: Don't like dried apricots? Substitute them with dried cranberries for a classic chocolate chip and cranberry combination!

PECAN SANDIES COOKIES

Yields: 12 small cookies | **Prep Time:** 10 minutes | **Inactive Time:** 30 minutes

INGREDIENTS

For the cookies:
1½ cups almond flour
½ cup medjool dates, pitted
2 tablespoons maple syrup
1 tablespoon coconut oil
½ teaspoon vanilla extract
⅛ teaspoon sea salt

For the add-in:
½ cup pecans, chopped

tip: Dress these cookies up by dipping them in melted chocolate or drizzling melted chocolate over the top!

DIRECTIONS

1. Prepare a cookie sheet lined with parchment paper. Set aside.

2. Add all ingredients for the cookies to a food processor and process until the dates are broken down into small pieces and everything is well combined, taking care to not over process.

3. Add the chopped pecan add-in and stir in by hand until they are evenly distributed.

4. Using a 1½-inch cookie scoop or a regular spoon, take one scoop of the mixture at a time and place it onto the prepared cookie sheet.

5. Flatten the cookies with the palm of your hand and smooth the edges with your fingertips.

6. Transfer the cookie sheet to the freezer for approximately 30 minutes, or until the cookies are firm.

7. Store in an air-tight container in the freezer or refrigerator until ready to serve, because the cookies will get soft if left out at room temperature.

DRIED BANANA + PEANUT BUTTER OAT COOKIES

Yields: 12 small cookies | **Prep Time:** 10 minutes | **Inactive Time:** 30 minutes

INGREDIENTS

1 cup gluten-free quick rolled oats
1 cup freeze-dried bananas
½ cup peanut butter
½ cup hemp seeds
¼ cup maple syrup
2 tablespoons coconut oil
½ teaspoon vanilla extract

tip: If you're in the mood for chocolate, you can add a chocolate drizzle over the top, or even dip the bottom half of the cookies in melted chocolate!

DIRECTIONS

1. Prepare a cookie sheet lined with parchment paper. Set aside.

2. Add all ingredients to a food processor and pulse about 10 to 12 times, or until the banana chips are broken down into small pieces and everything is well combined, taking care to not over process.

3. Take one spoonful of the mixture at a time, squeeze it tightly in your fist to make it compact, then flatten it between the palms of your hands into a round cookie shape about 2 inches in diameter. Place the cookies onto the prepared cookie sheet.

4. Transfer the cookie sheet to the freezer for approximately 30 minutes, or until the cookies are firm.

5. Store in an air-tight container in the freezer or refrigerator until ready to serve, because the cookies will get soft if left out at room temperature.

PECAN TURTLE CARAMEL THUMBPRINT COOKIES

Yields: 16 small cookies | **Prep Time:** 15 minutes | **Inactive Time:** 30 minutes

INGREDIENTS

For the cookies:
2 cups pecans
1 cup medjool dates, pitted
2 tablespoons coconut oil
2 tablespoons water
¼ teaspoon vanilla extract
⅛ teaspoon sea salt

For the caramel filling:
3 tablespoons almond butter
3 tablespoons maple syrup
1 tablespoon coconut oil
1 pinch sea salt

For the chocolate drizzle:
¼ cup semi-sweet mini chocolate chips
½ teaspoon coconut oil

DIRECTIONS

Prepare the cookies:

1. Prepare a cookie sheet lined with parchment paper. Set aside.

2. Add all ingredients for the cookies to a food processor and pulse about 10 to 12 times, or until the pecans and dates are broken down into small pieces and everything is well combined, taking care to not over process.

3. Take one spoonful of the mixture at a time, squeeze it tightly in your fist to make it compact, then gently roll it between the palms of your hands into a ball shape.

4. Flatten the ball shape between the palms of your hands into a round cookie shape about 2 inches in diameter. Place the cookies onto the prepared cookie sheet.

5. When finished preparing all the cookies, press down in the center of

(continued on next page)

each cookie with your thumb to form a "thumbprint" or a space deep enough to hold the caramel filling.

6. Transfer the cookie sheet to the freezer while you prepare the other steps.

Prepare the caramel filling:

1. Add all ingredients for the caramel to a small bowl and stir until everything is well combined and smooth.

Prepare the chocolate drizzle:

1. Add all ingredients for the chocolate drizzle to a small saucepan and melt on lowest heat, stirring until it is completely melted and smooth, taking care to not let it burn.

Assembly:

1. Remove the cookie sheet from the freezer.

2. Take a small spoonful of the caramel filling and fill in the center of each cookie.

3. Using a spoon, add the chocolate drizzle over the top of each cookie.

4. Return the cookie sheet to the freezer for approximately 30 minutes, or until the cookies and chocolate harden.

5. Store in an air-tight container in the freezer or refrigerator until ready to serve, because they will get soft if left out at room temperature.

STRAWBERRY CHOCOLATE CRISPY TREAT COOKIES

Yields: 9 cookies | **Prep Time:** 15 minutes | **Inactive Time:** 60 minutes

INGREDIENTS

For the cookies:
1 cup cashew butter
½ cup maple syrup
¼ cup cacao powder
¼ cup coconut oil
1 teaspoon vanilla extract

For the add-ins:
4 cups brown rice crisps cereal
2 cups freeze-dried strawberries, broken
    into tiny pieces

For the chocolate drizzle:
¼ cup semi-sweet mini chocolate chips
½ teaspoon coconut oil

DIRECTIONS

Prepare the cookies:

1. Prepare a cookie sheet lined with parchment paper. Set aside.

2. Add all ingredients for the cookies to a large bowl and stir until everything is well combined and smooth.

3. Add the brown rice crisps cereal and freeze-dried strawberry add-ins, and gently stir until they are evenly distributed.

4. Transfer the mixture to the prepared cookie sheet. Place an extra piece of parchment paper on top of the cookie mixture and press it down firmly and evenly into a 9 × 9 square shape, as compact as possible.

5. Place the cookie sheet in the freezer for approximately 30 minutes, or until firm.

6. Remove the cookie sheet from the freezer. Use the top rim of a small glass (about 3 inches in diameter) as a cookie

(continued on next page)

cutter and cut out 9 cookies from the frozen cookie mixture; remove any of the excess cookie mixture from the cookie sheet. Set aside.

Prepare the chocolate drizzle:

1. Add all ingredients for the chocolate drizzle to a small saucepan and melt on lowest heat until it is melted and smooth, stirring the entire time to make sure it doesn't burn.

2. Using a spoon, drizzle the melted chocolate evenly over the top of each cookie.

Assembly:

1. Return the cookie sheet to the freezer for approximately 30 minutes, or until the chocolate hardens.

2. Store in an air-tight container in the freezer or refrigerator until ready to serve, because the cookies will get soft if left out at room temperature.

tip: For a different variety, substitute freeze-dried raspberries for the freeze-dried strawberries.

2

bars

PECAN CRANBERRY BARS

Yields: 10 bars | **Prep Time:** 10 minutes | **Inactive Time:** 60 minutes

INGREDIENTS

1 cup medjool dates, pitted
2 cups pecans
1 cup hemp seeds
½ cup dried cranberries
1 tablespoon coconut oil
1 teaspoon vanilla extract
⅛ teaspoon sea salt

tip: You can make these fun by adding mini-chocolate chips in the mixture after you've processed all the other ingredients—just stir them in by hand. You can also drizzle melted chocolate over the top!

DIRECTIONS

1. Prepare an 8 × 8 baking dish lined with parchment paper. Set aside.

2. Add all ingredients to a food processor and process until the pecans, cranberries, and dates are broken down into small pieces and everything is well combined, taking care to not over process.

3. Transfer the mixture into the prepared baking dish and spread it evenly on the bottom of the dish. Place an extra piece of parchment paper on top of the mixture and press it down very tight and compact.

4. Place the baking dish in the freezer for approximately 60 minutes, or until the bars are firm.

5. Remove the baking dish from the freezer and cut into 10 bars or 20 squares.

6. Store in an air-tight container in the freezer or refrigerator until ready to serve, because the bars will get soft if left out at room temperature.

CRISPY CHOCOLATE TAHINI BARS

Yields: 10 bars | **Prep Time:** 10 minutes | **Inactive Time:** 60 minutes

INGREDIENTS

1½ cups gluten-free quick rolled oats
1 cup brown rice crisps cereal
1 cup medjool dates, pitted
½ cup almonds
½ cup tahini
¼ cup cacao powder
⅓ cup maple syrup
1 teaspoon vanilla extract
½ teaspoon ground cinnamon
¼ teaspoon sea salt

DIRECTIONS

1. Prepare an 8 × 8 baking dish lined with parchment paper. Set aside.

2. Add all ingredients to a food processor and process until the almonds and dates are broken down into small pieces and everything is well combined, taking care to not over process.

3. Transfer the mixture into the prepared baking dish and spread it evenly on the bottom of the dish. Place an extra piece of parchment paper on top of the mixture and press it down very tight and compact.

4. Place the baking dish in the freezer for approximately 60 minutes, or until the bars are firm.

5. Remove the baking dish from the freezer and cut into 10 bars or 20 squares.

6. Store in an air-tight container in the freezer or refrigerator until ready to serve, because the bars will get soft if left out at room temperature.

BLUEBERRY ALMOND GRANOLA BARS

Yields: 10 bars | **Prep Time:** 10 minutes | **Inactive Time:** 60 minutes

INGREDIENTS

For the bars:
2 cups gluten-free quick rolled oats
1 cup freeze-dried blueberries
1 cup cashew butter
½ cup maple syrup
¼ cup coconut oil
2 teaspoons vanilla extract
⅛ teaspoon sea salt

For the add-in:
½ cup almonds

DIRECTIONS

Prepare the add-in:

1. Add the almonds to a food processor and pulse 10 to 12 times, or until they are broken down into small pieces, taking care to not over process. Set aside.

Prepare the bars:

1. Prepare an 8 × 8 baking dish lined with parchment paper. Set aside.

2. Add all ingredients for the bars to a medium-sized bowl and stir until everything is well combined.

3. Add the chopped almond add-in and stir in by hand until they are evenly distributed.

4. Transfer the mixture into the prepared baking dish and spread it evenly on the bottom of the dish. Place an extra piece of parchment paper on top of the bar mixture and press it down very tight and compact.

5. Place the baking dish in the freezer for approximately 60 minutes, or until the bars are firm.

6. Remove the baking dish from the freezer and cut into 10 bars or 20 squares.

7. Store in an air-tight container in the freezer or refrigerator until ready to serve, because the bars will get soft if left out at room temperature.

CHOCOLATE ALMOND OAT BARS

Yields: 10 bars | **Prep Time:** 10 minutes | **Inactive Time:** 60 minutes

INGREDIENTS

1 cup gluten-free quick rolled oats
1 cup almonds
½ cup almond butter
½ cup medjool dates, pitted
¼ cup maple syrup
¼ cup + 2 tablespoons coconut oil
⅓ cup cacao powder
1 teaspoon vanilla extract
⅛ teaspoon sea salt

DIRECTIONS

1. Prepare an 8 × 8 baking dish lined with parchment paper. Set aside.

2. Add all ingredients to a food processor and process until the almonds and dates are broken down into small pieces and everything is well combined, taking care to not over process.

3. Transfer the mixture into the prepared baking dish and spread it evenly on the bottom of the dish. Place an extra piece of parchment paper on top of the mixture and press it down very tight and compact.

4. Place the baking dish in the freezer for approximately 60 minutes, or until the bars are firm.

5. Remove the baking dish from the freezer and cut into 10 bars or 20 squares.

6. Store in an air-tight container in the freezer or refrigerator until ready to serve, because the bars will get soft if left out at room temperature.

PEANUT BUTTER OAT BARS

Yields: 10 bars | **Prep Time:** 10 minutes | **Inactive Time:** 60 minutes

INGREDIENTS

2 cups gluten-free quick rolled oats
1 cup peanut butter
½ cup coconut oil
¼ cup maple syrup
1 teaspoon vanilla extract
⅛ teaspoon sea salt

DIRECTIONS

1. Prepare an 8 × 8 baking dish lined with parchment paper. Set aside.

2. Add all ingredients to a food processor and process until everything is well combined, taking care to not over process.

3. Transfer the mixture into the prepared baking dish and spread it evenly on the bottom of the dish. Place an extra piece of parchment paper on top of the mixture and press it down very tight and compact.

4. Place the baking dish in the freezer for approximately 60 minutes, or until the bars are firm.

5. Remove the baking dish from the freezer and cut into 10 bars or 20 squares.

6. Store in an air-tight container in the freezer or refrigerator until ready to serve, because the bars will get soft if left out at room temperature.

COCONUT + HAZELNUT ALMOND BARS

Yields: 10 bars | **Prep Time:** 10 minutes | **Inactive Time:** 60 minutes

INGREDIENTS
1 cup hazelnuts
1 cup almonds
1 cup unsweetened shredded coconut
1 cup medjool dates, pitted
¼ cup maple syrup
3 tablespoons coconut oil
2 tablespoons hemp seeds
2 teaspoons vanilla extract
¼ teaspoon sea salt

tip: Want to try a chocolate version? Add ¼ cup cacao powder to the mixture when mixing it in the food processor or drizzle melted chocolate over the top of the bars!

DIRECTIONS

1. Prepare an 8 × 8 baking dish lined with parchment paper. Set aside.

2. Add all ingredients to a food processor and process until the hazelnuts, almonds, and dates are broken down into small pieces and everything is well combined, taking care to not over process.

3. Transfer the mixture into the prepared baking dish and spread it evenly on the bottom of the dish. Place an extra piece of parchment paper on top of the mixture and press it down very tight and compact.

4. Place the baking dish in the freezer for approximately 60 minutes, or until the bars are firm.

5. Remove the baking dish from the freezer and cut into 10 bars or 20 squares.

6. Store in an air-tight container in the freezer or refrigerator until ready to serve, because the bars will get soft if left out at room temperature.

RASPBERRY PECAN FUDGE BARS

Yields: 6 bars | **Prep Time:** 10 minutes | **Inactive Time:** 60 minutes

INGREDIENTS

For the bars:
½ cup coconut oil
¼ cup maple syrup
¼ cup hemp seeds
2 tablespoons almond butter
2 tablespoons cacao powder
1 teaspoon vanilla extract
⅛ teaspoon sea salt

For the add-ins:
1 cup freeze-dried raspberries
1 cup pecans, chopped

For the garnish:
½ cup freeze-dried raspberries
½ cup pecans, chopped

DIRECTIONS

1. Prepare a 9 × 5 loaf pan dish lined with parchment paper. Set aside.

2. Add all ingredients for the bars to a medium-sized bowl and stir until well combined.

3. Add the freeze-dried raspberry and chopped pecan add-ins to the bowl and gently stir until they are evenly distributed.

4. Transfer the mixture into the prepared loaf pan and spread it evenly on the bottom of the pan.

5. Sprinkle the freeze-dried raspberry and chopped pecan garnish evenly over the top of the bars and gently pat them down so they are slightly embedded into the bars.

6. Place the baking dish in the freezer for approximately 60 minutes, or until the bars are firm.

7. Remove the loaf pan from the freezer and cut into 6 bars or 12 squares.

8. Store in an air-tight container in the freezer or refrigerator until ready to serve, because the bars will get soft if left out at room temperature.

TRIPLE SEED PISTACHIO BARS

Yields: 10 bars | **Prep Time:** 10 minutes | **Inactive Time:** 60 minutes

INGREDIENTS

For the bars:
1 cup medjool dates, pitted
½ cup tahini
½ cup almond butter
½ cup pistachios
½ cup hemp seeds
½ cup sesame seeds
¼ cup chia seeds
2 tablespoons coconut oil
⅛ teaspoon sea salt

For the pistachio garnish:
¼ cup pistachios, chopped

For the chocolate topping:
1 cup semi-sweet mini chocolate chips
1 tablespoon coconut oil

DIRECTIONS

Prepare the pistachio garnish:

1. Place the pistachios on a flat surface, like a countertop, and using the flat side of a butter knife, crush the pistachios into tiny pieces, as small as possible. Set aside.

Prepare the bars:

1. Prepare an 8 × 8 baking dish lined with parchment paper. Set aside.

2. Add all ingredients for the bars to a food processor and process until the pistachios and dates are broken down into small pieces and everything is well combined, taking care to not over process.

3. Transfer the mixture into the prepared baking dish and spread it evenly on the bottom of the dish. Place an extra piece of parchment paper on top of the bar mixture and press it down very tight and compact. Set aside.

(continued on next page)

Prepare the chocolate topping:

1. Add all ingredients for the chocolate topping to a small saucepan and melt on lowest heat, stirring until it is completely melted and smooth, taking care to not let it burn.

2. Pour the chocolate topping evenly over the top of the bars.

3. Sprinkle the pistachio garnish evenly over the top of the chocolate topping and gently pat them down so it's slightly embedded into the chocolate topping.

Assembly:

1. Place the baking dish in the freezer for approximately 60 minutes, or until the bars are firm.

2. Remove the baking dish from the freezer and cut into 10 bars or 20 squares.

3. Store in an air-tight container in the freezer or refrigerator until ready to serve, because the bars will get soft if left out at room temperature.

ALMOND + COCONUT FLAKE BARS

Yields: 10 bars | **Prep Time:** 10 minutes | **Inactive Time:** 60 minutes

INGREDIENTS

For the bars:
4 cups large coconut flakes
1 cup almonds
1 cup medjool dates, pitted
2 tablespoons cashew butter
2 tablespoons coconut oil
2 teaspoons vanilla extract

For the chocolate drizzle:
½ cup semi-sweet chocolate chips
1 teaspoon coconut oil

For the garnish:
2 tablespoons large coconut flakes
½ cup almonds, chopped

DIRECTIONS

Prepare the bars:

1. Prepare an 8 × 8 baking dish lined with parchment paper. Set aside.

2. Add all ingredients for the bars to a food processor and process until the almonds and dates are broken down into small pieces and everything is well combined, taking care to not over process.

3. Transfer the mixture into the prepared baking dish and spread it evenly on the bottom of the dish. Place an extra piece of parchment paper on top of the bar mixture and press it down very tight and compact. Set aside.

Prepare the chocolate drizzle:

1. Add all ingredients for the chocolate drizzle to a small saucepan and melt on lowest heat, stirring until it is completely melted and smooth, taking care to not let it burn.

(continued on next page)

2. Sprinkle the coconut flakes and almond garnish over the top of the bars.

3. Using a spoon, drizzle the melted chocolate evenly over the top of the coconut flakes.

Assembly:

1. Place the baking dish in the freezer for approximately 60 minutes, or until the bars are firm.

2. Remove the baking dish from the freezer and cut into 10 bars or 20 squares.

3. Store in an air-tight container in the freezer or refrigerator until ready to serve, because the bars will get soft if left out at room temperature.

PEANUT + TAHINI HEMP SEED BARS

Yields: 10 bars | **Prep Time:** 10 minutes | **Inactive Time:** 60 minutes

INGREDIENTS

For the bars:
1 cup hemp seeds
1 cup medjool dates, pitted
½ cup tahini
½ cup peanut butter
½ cup peanuts
2 tablespoons coconut oil
⅛ teaspoon sea salt

For the add-ins:
½ cup semi-sweet mini chocolate chips
½ cups peanuts

For the chocolate topping:
½ cup semi-sweet chocolate chips
2 tablespoons peanut butter

For the garnish:
½ cup peanuts

DIRECTIONS

Prepare the bars:

1. Prepare an 8 × 8 baking dish lined with parchment paper. Set aside.

2. Add all ingredients for the bars to a food processor and process until the peanuts and dates are broken down into small pieces and everything is well combined, taking care to not over process.

3. Add the peanut and chocolate chip add-ins to the food processor and stir in by hand until they are evenly distributed.

4. Transfer the mixture into the prepared baking dish and spread it evenly on the bottom of the dish. Place an extra piece of parchment paper on top of the bar mixture and press it down very tight and compact. Set aside.

Prepare the chocolate topping:

1. Add all ingredients for the chocolate topping to a small saucepan and

(continued on next page)

melt on lowest heat, stirring until it is completely melted and smooth, taking care to not let it burn.

2. Pour the chocolate topping evenly over the top of the bars.

3. Sprinkle the peanut garnish evenly over the chocolate topping and gently pat it down so it's slightly embedded into the chocolate topping.

Assembly:

1. Place the baking dish in the freezer for approximately 60 minutes, or until the bars are firm.

2. Remove the baking dish from the freezer and cut into 10 bars or 20 squares.

3. Store in an air-tight container in the freezer or refrigerator until ready to serve, because the bars will get soft if left out at room temperature.

CRISPY HAZELNUT BARS

Yields: 10 bars | **Prep Time:** 10 minutes | **Inactive Time:** 60 minutes

INGREDIENTS

For the bars:
3 cups brown rice crisps cereal
1 cup medjool dates, pitted
½ cup hazelnuts
½ cup cashew butter
½ cup coconut oil
¼ teaspoon ground cinnamon
¼ teaspoon sea salt

For the hazelnut garnish:
¼ cup hazelnuts, chopped

For the chocolate drizzle:
¼ cup semi-sweet mini chocolate chips
½ teaspoon coconut oil

DIRECTIONS

Prepare the hazelnut garnish:

1. Place the hazelnuts on a flat surface, like a countertop, and using the flat side of a butter knife, crush the hazelnuts into tiny pieces. Set aside.

Prepare the bars:

1. Prepare an 8 × 8 baking dish lined with parchment paper. Set aside.

2. Add all ingredients for the bars to a food processor and process until the hazelnuts and dates are broken down into small pieces and everything is well combined, taking care to not over process.

3. Transfer the mixture into the prepared baking dish and spread it evenly on the bottom of the dish. Place an extra piece of parchment paper on top of the bar mixture and press it down very tight and compact. Set aside.

Prepare the chocolate drizzle:

1. Add all ingredients for the chocolate drizzle to a small saucepan and melt on

(continued on next page)

lowest heat, stirring until it is completely melted and smooth, taking care to not let it burn.

2. Using a spoon, drizzle the melted chocolate evenly over the top of the bars.

3. Sprinkle the hazelnut garnish evenly over the top of the melted chocolate and gently pat them down so they are slightly embedded into the melted chocolate.

Assembly:

1. Place the baking dish in the freezer for approximately 60 minutes, or until the bars are firm.

2. Remove the baking dish from the freezer and cut into 10 bars or 20 squares.

3. Store in an air-tight container in the freezer or refrigerator until ready to serve, because the bars will get soft if left out at room temperature.

CRANBERRY + CASHEW CHIA SEED BARS

Yields: 10 bars | **Prep Time:** 10 minutes | **Inactive Time:** 60 minutes

INGREDIENTS

For the bars:
2 cups cashews
1 cup medjool dates, pitted
¼ cup cashew butter
¼ cup dried cranberries
¼ cup chia seeds
¼ cup coconut oil
1 teaspoon vanilla extract
¼ teaspoon sea salt

For the add-in:
½ cup semi-sweet mini chocolate chips

DIRECTIONS

1. Prepare an 8 × 8 baking dish lined with parchment paper. Set aside.

2. Add all ingredients for the bars to a food processor and process until the cashews, cranberries, and dates are broken down into small pieces and everything is well combined, taking care to not over process.

3. Add the chocolate chip add-in and stir in by hand until they are evenly distributed.

4. Transfer the mixture into the prepared baking dish and spread it evenly on the bottom of the dish. Place an extra piece of parchment paper on top of the mixture and press it down very tight and compact.

5. Place the baking dish in the freezer for approximately 60 minutes, or until the bars are firm.

6. Remove the baking dish from the freezer and cut into 10 bars or 20 squares.

7. Store in an air-tight container in the freezer or refrigerator until ready to serve, because the bars will get soft if left out at room temperature.

3

balls

CRANBERRY + PISTACHIO BALLS

Yields: 8 balls | **Prep Time:** 10 minutes | **Inactive Time:** 30 minutes

INGREDIENTS

For the balls:
1 cup unsweetened shredded coconut
2 tablespoons maple syrup
1 tablespoon cashew butter
½ teaspoon vanilla extract

For the add-ins:
½ cup cashews
⅓ cup pistachios
⅓ cup dried cranberries

For the garnish:
½ cup unsweetened shredded coconut

DIRECTIONS

Prepare the add-ins:

1. Add the cashew, pistachio, and dried cranberry add-ins to a food processor and pulse about 10 to 12 times, or until they are broken down into small pieces and everything is well combined, taking care to not over process. Set aside.

Prepare the balls:

1. Prepare a cookie sheet lined with parchment paper. Set aside.

2. Add all ingredients for the balls to a food processor and process until everything is well combined.

3. Add the chopped cashew, pistachio, and dried cranberry add-ins to the food processor and stir in by hand until they are evenly distributed.

4. Take one handful of the mixture at a time, squeeze it tightly in your fist to make it compact, then roll it between the palms of your hands into a ball shape.

5. Toss each ball in a small bowl with the unsweetened shredded coconut garnish until they are completely covered. Place the balls onto the prepared cookie sheet.

6. Transfer the cookie sheet to the freezer for approximately 30 minutes, or until the balls are firm.

7. Store in an air-tight container in the freezer or refrigerator until ready to serve, because the balls will get soft if left out at room temperature.

CASHEW + CHIA SEED COCONUT BALLS

Yields: 14 balls | **Prep Time:** 10 minutes | **Inactive Time:** 30 minutes

INGREDIENTS

1 cup cashews
1 cup medjool dates, pitted
⅓ cup unsweetened shredded coconut
2 tablespoons chia seeds
1 tablespoon coconut oil
1 teaspoon vanilla extract

DIRECTIONS

1. Prepare a cookie sheet lined with parchment paper. Set aside.

2. Add all ingredients to a food processor and process until the cashews and dates are broken down into small pieces and everything is well combined, taking care to not over process.

3. Take one handful of the mixture at a time, squeeze it tightly in your fist to make it compact, then roll it between the palms of your hands into a ball shape. Place the balls onto the prepared cookie sheet.

4. Transfer the cookie sheet to the freezer for approximately 30 minutes, or until the balls are firm.

5. Store in an air-tight container in the freezer or refrigerator until ready to serve, because the balls will get soft if left out at room temperature.

LEMON GINGER SESAME SEED BALLS

Yields: 16 balls | **Prep Time:** 10 minutes | **Inactive Time:** 30 minutes

INGREDIENTS

For the balls:
2 cups + 2 tablespoons almond flour
6 tablespoons sesame seeds
¼ cup maple syrup
3 tablespoons lemon juice
2 tablespoons coconut oil
1 teaspoon ground ginger
1 pinch sea salt

For the garnish:
¼ cup sesame seeds

DIRECTIONS

1. Prepare a cookie sheet lined with parchment paper. Set aside.

2. Add all ingredients for the balls to a food processor and process until everything is well combined.

3. Take one handful of the mixture at a time and roll it between the palms of your hands into a ball shape.

4. Toss each ball in a small bowl with the sesame seed garnish until they are completely covered. Place the balls onto the prepared cookie sheet.

5. Transfer the cookie sheet to the freezer for approximately 30 minutes, or until the balls are firm.

6. Store in an air-tight container in the freezer or refrigerator until ready to serve, because the balls will get soft if left out at room temperature.

CHOCOLATE CHIP PECAN + OAT COOKIE DOUGH BALLS

Yields: 22 balls | **Prep Time:** 10 minutes | **Inactive Time:** 30 minutes

INGREDIENTS

For the balls:
1 cup cashew butter
1 cup almond flour
½ cup gluten-free quick rolled oats
1 teaspoon vanilla extract
¼ teaspoon sea salt

For the add-ins:
1 cup pecans, chopped
1 cup semi-sweet mini chocolate chips

DIRECTIONS

1. Prepare a cookie sheet lined with parchment paper. Set aside.

2. Add all ingredients for the balls to a food processor and process until everything is well combined.

3. Add the pecan and chocolate chip add-ins to the food processor and stir in by hand until they are evenly distributed.

4. Take one handful of the mixture at a time, squeeze it tightly in your fist to make it compact, then roll it between the palms of your hands into a ball shape. Place the balls onto the prepared cookie sheet.

5. Transfer the cookie sheet to the freezer for approximately 30 minutes, or until the balls are firm.

6. Store in an air-tight container in the freezer or refrigerator until ready to serve, because the balls will get soft if left out at room temperature.

WALNUT BROWNIE FUDGE BALLS

INGREDIENTS

1 cup walnuts
1 cup medjool dates, pitted
¼ cup cacao powder
2 tablespoons almond flour
1 tablespoon coconut oil
½ teaspoon vanilla extract

tip: If you want to dress these up, drizzle melted chocolate over each ball then sprinkle chopped walnuts on top of the chocolate before adding them to the freezer!

DIRECTIONS

1. Prepare a cookie sheet lined with parchment paper. Set aside.

2. Add all ingredients to a food processor and process until the walnuts and dates are broken down into small pieces and everything is well combined, taking care to not over process.

3. Take one handful of the mixture at a time, squeeze it tightly in your fist to make it compact, then roll it between the palms of your hands into a ball shape. Place the balls onto the prepared cookie sheet.

4. Transfer the cookie sheet to the freezer for approximately 30 minutes, or until the balls are firm.

5. Store in an air-tight container in the freezer or refrigerator until ready to serve, because the balls will get soft if left out at room temperature.

CHOCOLATE COVERED PUMPKIN BALLS

Yields: 14 balls | **Prep Time:** 10 minutes | **Inactive Time:** 60 minutes

INGREDIENTS

For the balls:

1½ cups brown rice crisps cereal
½ cup medjool dates, pitted
¼ cup almond butter
¼ cup pumpkin puree
2 tablespoons coconut oil
½ teaspoon pumpkin spice
½ teaspoon vanilla extract

For the chocolate coating:

¼ cup semi-sweet mini chocolate chips
½ teaspoon coconut oil
½ teaspoon almond butter

DIRECTIONS

Prepare the balls:

1. Prepare a cookie sheet lined with parchment paper. Set aside.

2. Add all ingredients for the balls to a food processor and pulse about 8 to 10 times, or until the dates are broken down into small pieces and everything is well combined, taking care to not over process.

3. Take one handful of the mixture at a time, squeeze it tightly in your fist to make it compact, then roll it between the palms of your hands into a ball shape. Place the balls onto the prepared cookie sheet. Set aside.

Prepare the chocolate coating:

1. Add all ingredients for the chocolate coating to a small saucepan and melt on lowest heat until it is melted and smooth, stirring the entire time to make sure it doesn't burn.

2. Dip each ball into the chocolate coating until the ball is completely covered; use a fork to flip them over and to allow the excess chocolate to drip off. Return the balls onto the prepared cookie sheet.

Assembly:

1. Transfer the cookie sheet to the refrigerator for approximately 60 minutes, or until the balls are firm and the chocolate is hardened.

2. Store in an air-tight container in the freezer or refrigerator until ready to serve, because the balls will get soft if left out at room temperature.

RASPBERRY + DATE BALLS

Yields: 7 balls | **Prep Time:** 10 minutes | **Inactive Time:** 30 minutes

INGREDIENTS

For the balls:
1 cup freeze-dried raspberries
1 cup medjool dates, pitted
2 tablespoons cashew butter
1 teaspoon vanilla extract
1 pinch sea salt

For the garnish:
¼ cup freeze-dried raspberries

DIRECTIONS

Prepare the garnish:

1. Add the freeze-dried raspberry garnish to a food processor and process until they are broken down into a fine powder.

2. Transfer to a small bowl. Set aside.

Prepare the balls:

1. Prepare a cookie sheet lined with parchment paper. Set aside.

2. Add all ingredients for the balls to a food processor and process until the dates are broken down into small pieces and everything is well combined, taking care to not over process.

3. Take out a handful of the mixture at a time, squeeze it tightly in your fist to make it compact, then roll it between the palms of your hands into a ball shape.

4. Toss each ball in the small bowl with the freeze-dried raspberry garnish until they are completely covered. Place the balls onto the prepared cookie sheet.

5. Transfer the cookie sheet to the freezer for approximately 30 minutes, or until the balls are firm.

6. Store in an air-tight container in the freezer or refrigerator until ready to serve, because the balls will get soft if left out at room temperature.

tip: You can use your favorite freeze-dried fruit in this recipe like blueberries, strawberries, mango, apple, peach, or bananas!

CHEWY OATMEAL COOKIE BALLS

Yields: 10 balls | **Prep Time:** 10 minutes | **Inactive Time:** 30 minutes

INGREDIENTS

1 cup gluten-free quick oats
1 cup medjool dates, pitted
1 tablespoon coconut oil
1 tablespoon water
½ teaspoon ground cinnamon
¼ teaspoon vanilla extract
⅛ teaspoon sea salt

DIRECTIONS

1. Prepare a cookie sheet lined with parchment paper. Set aside.

2. Add all ingredients to a food processor and process until the dates are broken down into small pieces and everything is well combined, taking care to not over process.

3. Take one handful of the mixture at a time, squeeze it tightly in your fist to make it compact, then roll it between the palms of your hands into a ball shape. Place the balls onto the prepared cookie sheet.

4. Transfer the cookie sheet to the freezer for approximately 30 minutes, or until the balls are firm.

5. Store in an air-tight container in the freezer or refrigerator until ready to serve, because the balls will get soft if left out at room temperature.

MIXED NUT + SEED BALLS

Yields: 20 balls | **Prep Time:** 10 minutes | **Inactive Time:** 30 minutes

INGREDIENTS

1 cup medjool dates, pitted
½ cup almonds
½ cup hazelnuts
½ cup pumpkin seeds
½ cup gluten-free quick rolled oats
¼ cup chia seeds
¼ cup almond butter
2 tablespoons maple syrup
½ teaspoon vanilla extract
¼ teaspoon ground cinnamon
⅛ teaspoon sea salt

DIRECTIONS

1. Prepare a cookie sheet lined with parchment paper. Set aside.

2. Add all ingredients to a food processor and process until the almonds, hazelnuts, pumpkin seeds, and dates are broken down into small pieces and everything is well combined, taking care to not over process.

3. Take one handful of the mixture at a time, squeeze it tightly in your fist to make it compact, then roll it between the palms of your hands into a ball shape. Place the balls onto the prepared cookie sheet.

4. Transfer the cookie sheet to the freezer for approximately 30 minutes, or until the balls are firm.

5. Store in an air-tight container in the freezer or refrigerator until ready to serve, because the balls will get soft if left out at room temperature.

HAZELNUT CARAMEL BALLS

Yields: 8 balls | **Prep Time:** 10 minutes | **Inactive Time:** 30 minutes

INGREDIENTS

For the balls:
1 cup medjool dates, pitted
½ cup hazelnuts
1 tablespoon coconut oil
½ teaspoon vanilla extract
1 pinch sea salt

For the hazelnut garnish:
¼ cup hazelnuts, chopped

For the chocolate coating:
½ cup semi-sweet mini chocolate chips
1 teaspoon coconut oil

DIRECTIONS

Prepare the hazelnut garnish:

1. Place the hazelnuts on a flat surface, like a countertop, and using the flat side of a butter knife, crush the hazelnuts into tiny pieces, as small as possible.

2. Transfer to a small bowl and set aside.

Prepare the balls:

1. Prepare a cookie sheet lined with parchment paper. Set aside.

2. Add all ingredients for the balls to a food processor and process until the hazelnuts and dates are broken down into small pieces and everything is well combined, taking care to not over process.

3. Take one handful of the mixture at a time, squeeze it tightly in your fist to make it compact, then roll it between the palms of your hands into a ball shape. Place the balls onto the prepared cookie sheet. Set aside.

(continued on next page)

Prepare the chocolate coating:

1. Add all ingredients for the chocolate coating to a small saucepan and melt on lowest heat, stirring until it is completely melted and smooth, taking care to not let it burn.

2. Dip each ball into the chocolate coating until the ball is completely covered; use a fork to flip them over and to let the excess chocolate drip off. Place the balls back onto the cookie sheet.

3. Sprinkle the hazelnut garnish over the top of each ball.

Assembly:

1. Transfer the cookie sheet to the freezer for approximately 30 minutes, or until the balls are firm and the chocolate is hardened.

2. Store in an air-tight container in the freezer or refrigerator until ready to serve, because the balls will get soft if left out at room temperature.

CHOCOLATE PEANUT BUTTER CRISPY BALLS

Yields: 18 balls | **Prep Time:** 10 minutes | **Inactive Time:** 30 minutes

INGREDIENTS

For the balls:
1 cup peanut butter
1 cup medjool dates, pitted
¼ cup cacao powder
1 tablespoon coconut oil
1 tablespoon maple syrup
1 teaspoon vanilla extract

For the add-in:
2 cups brown rice crisps cereal

For the crispy coating:
1 cup brown rice crisps cereal

For the chocolate drizzle:
½ cup semi-sweet mini chocolate chips
1 teaspoon coconut oil

DIRECTIONS

Prepare the crispy coating:

1. Add the brown rice crispy cereal for the crispy coating to a food processor and pulse about 10 to 12 times, or until the brown rice crispy cereal is broken down into small pieces, taking care to not over process.

2. Transfer to a small bowl and set aside.

Prepare the balls:

1. Prepare a cookie sheet lined with parchment paper. Set aside.

2. Add all ingredients for the balls to a food processor and process until the dates are broken down into small pieces and everything is well combined, taking care to not over process.

3. Add the brown rice crisps cereal add-in to the food processor and pulse about 10 to 12 times, or until the brown rice crisps cereal is broken down into small pieces, taking care to not over process.

(continued on next page)

4. Take one handful of the mixture at a time, squeeze it tightly in your fist to make it compact, then roll it between the palms of your hands into a ball shape.

5. Toss each ball in the small bowl with the brown rice crispy cereal coating until they are completely covered. Place the balls onto the prepared cookie sheet. Set aside.

Prepare the chocolate drizzle:

1. Add all ingredients for the chocolate drizzle to a small saucepan and melt on lowest heat, stirring until it is completely melted and smooth, and taking care to not let it burn.

2. Using a spoon, drizzle the melted chocolate evenly over the top of each ball.

Assembly:

1. Transfer the cookie sheet to the freezer for approximately 30 minutes, or until the balls are firm and the chocolate is hardened.

2. Store in an air-tight container in the freezer or refrigerator until ready to serve, because the balls will get soft if left out at room temperature.

PISTACHIO SESAME SEED BALLS

Yields: 14 balls | **Prep Time:** 10 minutes | **Inactive Time:** 30 minutes

INGREDIENTS

½ cup pistachios
½ cup almond butter
½ cup sesame seeds
1 cup medjool dates, pitted
1 tablespoon coconut oil

DIRECTIONS

1. Prepare a cookie sheet lined with parchment paper. Set aside.

2. Add all ingredients to a food processor and process until the pistachios and dates are broken down into small pieces and everything is well combined, taking care to not over process.

3. Take one handful of the mixture at a time, squeeze it tightly in your fist to make it compact, then roll it between the palms of your hands into a ball shape. Place the balls onto the prepared cookie sheet.

4. Transfer the cookie sheet to the freezer for approximately 30 minutes, or until the balls are firm.

5. Store in an air-tight container in the freezer or refrigerator until ready to serve, because the balls will get soft if left out at room temperature.

4

dessert squares

CREAMY PUMPKIN SQUARES

Yields: 8 large squares | **Prep Time:** 10 minutes | **Inactive Time:** overnight

INGREDIENTS

For the crust layer:
1½ cups brown rice crisps cereal
¼ cup almond butter
½ cup medjool dates, pitted
2 tablespoons coconut oil
½ teaspoon vanilla extract
½ teaspoon pumpkin spice
⅛ teaspoon sea salt

For the pumpkin layer:
1 can pumpkin puree, 15-ounce can
1 can full-fat coconut milk, 13.5-ounce can
¼ cup cashew butter
¼ cup coconut oil
¼ cup maple syrup
1 teaspoon vanilla extract
½ teaspoon pumpkin spice
⅛ teaspoon sea salt

For the chocolate topping:
2 tablespoons almond butter
2 tablespoons maple syrup
2 tablespoons cacao powder
1 tablespoon coconut oil

DIRECTIONS

Prepare the crust layer:

1. Prepare a 9 × 5 loaf pan lined with parchment paper. Set aside.

2. Add all ingredients for the crust layer to a food processor and process until the brown rice crisps cereal and dates are broken down into small pieces and everything is well combined, taking care to not over process.

3. Transfer the mixture into the prepared loaf pan and spread it evenly on the bottom of the pan. Place an extra piece of parchment paper on top of the crust mixture and press it down very tight and compact. Set aside.

Prepare the pumpkin layer:

1. Add all ingredients for the pumpkin layer to food processor and process until everything is well combined and smooth.

2. Transfer the pumpkin layer mixture to the loaf pan and spread it evenly on top of the crust layer.

(continued on next page)

Prepare the chocolate topping:

1. Add all ingredients for the chocolate topping to a small bowl and stir until everything is well combined and smooth.

2. Pour the chocolate topping evenly over the top of the layers.

Assembly:

1. Place the loaf pan in the freezer overnight, or until the squares are firm.

2. Remove the loaf pan from the freezer and cut into 8 large squares.

3. Store in an air-tight container in the freezer until ready to serve, because the squares will get soft if left out at room temperature.

CHOCOLATE CHIP COOKIE DOUGH SQUARES

Yields: 8 large squares | **Prep Time:** 10 minutes | **Inactive Time:** overnight

INGREDIENTS

For the crust layer:
1 cup almonds
½ cup medjool dates, pitted
¼ cup cacao powder
2 tablespoons coconut oil
⅛ teaspoon sea salt

For the cookie dough layer:
1 can garbanzo beans, 15-ounce can;
    drained and rinsed
½ cup cashew butter
¼ cup almond flour
3 tablespoons maple syrup
1 tablespoon coconut oil
1 teaspoon vanilla extract
½ teaspoon sea salt
⅛ teaspoon ground cinnamon

For the add-in:
1 cup semi-sweet mini chocolate chips

For the chocolate topping:
½ cup semi-sweet mini chocolate chips
2 tablespoons almond butter
1 tablespoon coconut oil

DIRECTIONS

Prepare the crust layer:

1. Prepare a 9 × 5 loaf pan lined with parchment paper. Set aside.

2. Add all ingredients for the crust layer to a food processor and process until the almonds and dates are broken down into small pieces and everything is well combined, taking care to not over process.

3. Transfer the mixture into the prepared loaf pan and spread it evenly on the bottom of the pan. Place an extra piece of parchment paper on top of the crust mixture and press it down very tight and compact. Set aside.

Prepare the cookie dough layer:

1. Add all ingredients for the cookie dough layer to food processor and process until everything is well combined and smooth.

(continued on next page)

2. Add the chocolate chip add-in to the food processor and stir in by hand until it is evenly distributed.

3. Transfer the cookie dough mixture to the loaf pan and spread it evenly on top of the crust layer.

Prepare the chocolate topping:

1. Add all ingredients for the chocolate topping to a small saucepan and melt on lowest heat, stirring until it is completely melted and smooth, taking care to not let it burn.

2. Pour the chocolate topping evenly over the top of the cookie dough layer.

Assembly:

1. Place the loaf pan in the freezer overnight, or until the squares are firm.

2. Remove the loaf pan from the freezer and cut into 8 large squares.

3. Store in an air-tight container in the freezer or refrigerator until ready to serve, because the squares will get soft if left out at room temperature.

PEANUT BUTTER BROWNIE SQUARES

Yields: 16 squares | Prep Time: 10 minutes | Inactive Time: 60 minutes

INGREDIENTS

For the brownie layer:
1 cup medjool dates, pitted
½ cup cacao powder
½ cup sunflower seeds
½ cup hemp seeds
2 tablespoons coconut oil
1 teaspoon vanilla extract
⅛ teaspoon sea salt

For the peanut butter layer:
1 cup peanut butter
¼ cup maple syrup
¼ cup coconut oil
¼ cup coconut flour

DIRECTION

Prepare the brownie layer:

1. Prepare an 8 × 8 baking dish lined with parchment paper. Set aside.

2. Add all ingredients for the brownie layer to a food processor and process until the seeds and dates are broken down into small pieces and everything is well combined, taking care to not over process.

3. Transfer the mixture into the prepared baking dish and spread it evenly on the bottom of the dish. Place an extra piece of parchment paper on top of the brownie mixture and press it down very tight and compact. Set aside.

Prepare the peanut butter layer:

1. Add all ingredients for the peanut butter layer to a medium-sized bowl and stir until everything is well combined and smooth.

2. Transfer the peanut butter mixture to the baking dish and spread it evenly on top of the brownie layer.

3. Place the baking dish in the freezer for approximately 60 minutes, or until the squares are firm.

4. Remove the baking dish from the freezer and cut into 16 squares.

5. Store in an air-tight container in the freezer or refrigerator until ready to serve, because the squares will get soft if left out at room temperature.

LEMON SQUARES

Yields: 8 large squares | **Prep Time:** 10 minutes | **Inactive Time:** 1 hour + overnight

INGREDIENTS

For the crust layer:
1 cups walnuts
½ cup medjool dates, pitted
2 tablespoons coconut oil

For the lemon layer:
3 cups cashews, soaked for 1 hour and
  drained*
½ cup maple syrup
½ cup lemon juice
¼ cup coconut oil
½ teaspoon vanilla extract
⅛ teaspoon sea salt

tip: *To make sure the cheesecake filling is as smooth and creamy as possible, you will need to soak the cashews for at least 1 hour in a bowl of water, then drain and rinse before adding them to the food processor.

tip: You can customize this dessert by adding fresh blueberries, raspberries, or even blackberries over the top of each square before serving!

DIRECTIONS

Prepare the crust layer:

1. Prepare an 9 × 5 loaf pan lined with parchment paper. Set aside.

2. Add all ingredients for the crust layer to a food processor and process until the walnuts and dates are broken down into small pieces and everything is well combined, taking care to not over process.

3. Transfer the mixture into the prepared loaf pan and spread it evenly on the bottom of the pan. Place an extra piece of parchment paper on top of the crust mixture and press it down very tight and compact. Set aside.

Prepare the lemon layer:

1. Add all ingredients for the lemon layer to a food processor and process until the cashews are broken down and everything is creamy and smooth. This should take approximately 5 minutes, and you may have to stop and scrape the sides several times to help it along.

(continued on next page)

2. Transfer the lemon layer to the prepared loaf pan and spread it evenly on top of the crust layer.

3. Place the loaf pan in the freezer overnight, or until firm.

4. Remove the loaf pan from the freezer and cut into 8 large squares.

5. Store in an air-tight container in the freezer or refrigerator until ready to serve, because the squares will get soft if left out at room temperature.

POMEGRANATE + CARAMEL BROWNIE SQUARES

Yields: 10 small squares | **Prep Time:** 15 minutes | **Inactive Time:** 60 minutes

INGREDIENTS

For the brownie layer:
1 cup walnuts
¼ cup cacao powder
4 medjool dates, pitted
2 tablespoons coconut oil
⅛ teaspoon sea salt

For the pomegranate topping:
1 cup pomegranate seeds

For the caramel layer:
2 cups medjool dates, pitted
¼ cup coconut oil
2 tablespoons almond butter
2 teaspoons vanilla extract

For the chocolate drizzle:
¼ cup semi-sweet mini-chocolate chips
½ teaspoon coconut oil

DIRECTIONS

Prepare the brownie layer:

1. Prepare a 9 × 5 loaf pan lined with parchment paper. Set aside.

2. Add all ingredients for the brownie layer to a food processor and process until the walnuts and dates are broken down into small pieces and everything is well combined, taking care to not over process.

3. Transfer the mixture into the prepared loaf pan and spread it evenly on the bottom of the pan. Place an extra piece of parchment paper on top of the brownie mixture and press it down very tight and compact.

4. Place the loaf pan in the freezer to firm while you prepare the rest of the recipe.

Prepare the pomegranate topping:

1. Seed the pomegranate by scoring the outside with a sharp knife, without cutting all the way through. Use your hands to pry the pomegranate in half.

(continued on next page)

2. Place one of the halves face down in the palm of your hand and, using the other hand, tap the outside of the pomegranate with a spoon until the seeds fall out. Have a medium-sized bowl ready to catch the seeds. Set aside.

Prepare the caramel layer:

1. Add all ingredients for the caramel layer to a food processor and process until the dates are broken down into tiny pieces and everything is well combined, taking care to not over process.

Prepare the chocolate drizzle:

1. Add all ingredients for the chocolate drizzle to a small saucepan and melt on lowest heat, stirring until it is completely melted and smooth, taking care to not let it burn. Set aside.

Assembly:

1. Remove the loaf pan from the freezer. Transfer the caramel mixture into the loaf pan and spread it evenly on top of the brownie layer.

2. Sprinkle the pomegranate seed topping evenly on top of the caramel layer and gently pat it down so it's slightly embedded into the layer.

3. Using a spoon, drizzle the melted chocolate evenly over the top of the pomegranate seeds.

4. Place the loaf pan in the freezer for approximately 60 minutes, or until the squares are firm and the chocolate is hardened.

5. Remove the loaf pan from the freezer and cut into 10 small squares.

6. Store in an air-tight container in the freezer or refrigerator until ready to serve, because the squares will get soft if left out at room temperature.

CHOCOLATE PEANUT BUTTER LAYERED OAT SQUARES

Yields: 16 squares | **Prep Time:** 10 minutes | **Inactive Time:** 60 minutes

INGREDIENTS

For the oat layers:
3 cups gluten-free quick rolled oats
1 cup medjool dates, pitted
½ cup coconut oil
2 tablespoons maple syrup
½ teaspoon vanilla extract
¼ teaspoon sea salt

For the chocolate layer:
1 cup semi-sweet mini chocolate chips
1 cup peanut butter
1 tablespoon coconut oil

DIRECTIONS

Prepare the oat layers:

1. Prepare an 8 × 8 baking dish lined with parchment paper. Set aside.

2. Add all ingredients for the oat layers to a food processor and process until the dates are broken down into small pieces and everything is well combined, taking care to not over process. Set aside.

Prepare the chocolate layer:

1. Add all ingredients for the chocolate layer to a small saucepan and melt on lowest heat, stirring until it is completely melted and smooth, taking care to not let it burn.

Assembly:

1. Transfer half of the oat layer mixture to the prepared baking dish and spread it evenly on the bottom of the dish. Place an extra piece of parchment paper on top of the oat mixture and press it down very tight and compact.

(continued on next page)

2. Pour the chocolate layer mixture evenly over the top of the oat layer mixture, reserving a few tablespoons to drizzle on the top of the bars.

3. Using your hands, sprinkle the remaining half of the oat layer mixture evenly over the top of the chocolate layer and gently pat it down so it's slightly embedded into the chocolate layer.

4. Using a spoon, drizzle the remaining chocolate layer mixture evenly over the top of the squares.

5. Place the baking dish in the freezer for approximately 60 minutes, or until the squares are firm.

6. Remove the baking dish from the freezer and cut into 16 squares.

7. Store in an air-tight container in the freezer or refrigerator until ready to serve, because the squares will get soft if left out at room temperature.

NANAIMO SQUARES

Yields: 16 squares | **Prep Time:** 15 minutes | **Inactive Time:** 1 hour + overnight

INGREDIENTS

For the crust layer:
2 cups almonds
2 cups medjool dates, pitted
1 cup unsweetened shredded coconut
¼ cup cacao powder
3 tablespoons coconut oil
⅛ teaspoon sea salt

For the filling layer:
2 cups cashews, soaked for 1 hour and
    drained*
¼ cup maple syrup
1 teaspoon vanilla extract

For the chocolate topping:
1½ cups semi-sweet mini chocolate chips
1 tablespoon coconut oil

tip: *To make sure the cheesecake filling is as smooth and creamy as possible, you will need to soak the cashews for at least 1 hour in a bowl of water, then drain and rinse before adding them to the food processor.

DIRECTIONS

Prepare the crust layer:

1. Prepare an 8 × 8 baking dish lined with parchment paper. Set aside.

2. Add all ingredients for the crust layer to a food processor and process until the almonds and dates are broken down into small pieces and everything is well combined, taking care to not over process.

3. Transfer the mixture to the prepared baking dish and spread it evenly on the bottom of the dish. Place an extra piece of parchment paper on top of the crust mixture and press it down very tight and compact. Set aside.

Prepare the filling layer:

1. Add all ingredients for the filling layer to a food processor and process until the cashews are broken down and everything is creamy and smooth. This should take approximately 5 minutes, and you may have to stop and scrape the sides several times to help it along.

(continued on next page)

2. Transfer the mixture to the prepared baking dish and spread it evenly over the top of the crust layer with your hands, using wet fingertips to avoid sticking to the mixture.

Prepare the chocolate topping:

1. Add all ingredients for the chocolate topping to a small saucepan and melt on lowest heat, stirring until it is completely melted and smooth, taking care to not let it burn.

2. Pour the chocolate topping evenly over the top of the filling layer.

Assembly:

1. Place the baking dish in the freezer overnight, or until the squares are firm.

2. Remove the baking dish from the freezer and cut into 16 squares.

3. Store in an air-tight container in the freezer or refrigerator until ready to serve, because the squares will get soft if left out at room temperature.

CARAMEL PEANUT BUTTER CRISPY SQUARES

Yields: 16 squares | **Prep Time:** 10 minutes | **Inactive Time:** overnight

INGREDIENTS

For the peanut butter crispy layer:
3 cups brown rice crisps cereal
½ cup peanut butter
½ cup maple syrup
1 teaspoon vanilla extract
¼ teaspoon sea salt

For the caramel layer:
1 cup medjool dates, pitted
¼ cup water
1 tablespoon coconut oil
1 teaspoon vanilla extract
¼ teaspoon sea salt

For the chocolate topping:
1 cup semi-sweet mini chocolate chips
1 tablespoon peanut butter
1 tablespoon coconut oil

DIRECTIONS

Prepare the peanut butter crispy layer:

1. Prepare an 8 × 8 baking dish lined with parchment paper. Set aside.

2. Add all ingredients for the peanut butter crispy layer to a food processor and process until the cereal is broken down into small pieces and everything is well combined, taking care to not over process.

3. Transfer the mixture to the prepared baking dish and spread it evenly on the bottom of the dish. Place an extra piece of parchment paper on top of the peanut butter crispy mixture and press it down very tight and compact. Set aside.

Prepare the caramel layer:

1. Add all ingredients for the caramel layer to a food processor and process until the dates are broken down into small pieces and everything is well combined.

(continued on next page)

2. Transfer the mixture to the baking dish and spread it evenly over the top of the peanut butter crispy layer.

Prepare the chocolate topping:

1. Add all ingredients for the chocolate topping to a small saucepan and melt on lowest heat, stirring until it is completely melted and smooth, taking care to not let it burn.

2. Pour the chocolate topping evenly over the top of the caramel layer.

Assembly:

1. Place the baking dish in the freezer overnight, or until the squares are firm.

2. Remove the baking dish from the freezer and cut into 16 squares or 8 large bars.

3. Store in an air-tight container in the freezer or refrigerator until ready to serve, because the squares will get soft if left out at room temperature.

7-LAYER MAGIC BAR SQUARES

Yields: 8 small squares | **Prep Time:** 10 minutes | **Inactive Time:** 60 minutes

INGREDIENTS

For the cookie layer:
1 cup almond flour
¼ cup maple syrup
¼ cup coconut oil
1 tablespoon coconut flour
¼ teaspoon vanilla extract
⅛ teaspoon sea salt

For the chocolate caramel topping:
¼ cup coconut oil
¼ cup maple syrup
2 tablespoons cacao powder
2 tablespoons almond butter
⅛ teaspoon sea salt

For the add-ins:
¼ cup semi-sweet mini chocolate chips
¼ cup pecans, chopped
¼ cup walnuts, chopped
¼ cup pistachios, chopped

For the garnish:
2 tablespoons unsweetened shredded
  coconut

DIRECTIONS

Prepare the cookie layer:

1. Prepare a 9 × 5 loaf pan lined with parchment paper. Set aside.

2. Add all ingredients for the cookie layer to a medium-sized bowl and stir until everything is well combined.

3. Transfer the mixture into the prepared loaf pan and spread it evenly on the bottom of the pan. Place an extra piece of parchment paper on top of the cookie mixture and press it down very tight and compact. Set aside.

Prepare the chocolate caramel topping:

1. Add all ingredients for the chocolate caramel topping to a medium-sized bowl and stir until everything is well combined and smooth.

2. Add all ingredients for the add-ins to the bowl with the chocolate caramel topping and stir until everything is well combined.

(continued on next page)

3. Pour the chocolate caramel topping mixture into the loaf pan and spread it evenly over the cookie layer.

4. Sprinkle the unsweetened shredded coconut garnish evenly over the top of the chocolate caramel topping.

Assembly:

1. Place the loaf pan in the freezer for approximately 60 minutes, or until the squares firm.

2. Remove the loaf pan from the freezer and cut into 8 small squares.

3. Store in an air-tight container in the freezer or refrigerator until ready to serve, because the squares will get soft if left out at room temperature.

CHOCOLATE PECAN PIE SQUARES

Yields: 8 small squares | **Prep Time:** 10 minutes | **Inactive Time:** 2 hours

INGREDIENTS

For the pecan layer:
1 cup medjool dates, pitted
½ cup almond butter
1 teaspoon vanilla extract
⅛ teaspoon ground cinnamon
⅛ teaspoon sea salt

For the add-in:
1 cup pecans

For the chocolate drizzle:
¼ cup semi-sweet mini chocolate chips
1 tablespoon almond butter
½ teaspoon coconut oil

For the garnish:
½ cup pecans, chopped

DIRECTIONS

Prepare the pecan layer:

1. Prepare a 9 × 5 loaf pan lined with parchment paper. Set aside.

2. Add all ingredients for the pecan layer to a food processor and process until the dates are broken down into small pieces and everything is well combined, taking care to not over process.

3. Add the pecan add-in to the food processor and pulse 10 to 12 times, or until the pecans are broken into small pieces and everything is well combined, taking care to not over process.

4. Transfer the mixture to the prepared loaf pan and spread it evenly on the bottom of the pan. Place an extra piece of parchment paper on top of the pecan mixture and press it down very tight and compact. Set aside.

Prepare the chocolate drizzle:

1. Add all ingredients for the chocolate drizzle to a small saucepan and melt on

(continued on next page)

lowest heat, stirring until it is completely melted and smooth, taking care to not let it burn.

2. Using a spoon, drizzle the melted chocolate evenly over the top of the pecan layer.

3. Sprinkle the chopped pecan garnish evenly over the top of the melted chocolate and gently pat it down so it's slightly embedded into the melted chocolate.

Assembly:

1. Place the loaf pan in the freezer for approximately 2 hours, or until the squares are firm and the chocolate is hardened.

2. Remove the loaf pan from the freezer and cut into 8 small squares.

3. Store in an air-tight container in the freezer or refrigerator until ready to serve, because the squares will get soft if left out at room temperature.

PEANUT BUTTER + CHIA JAM SWIRL SQUARES

Yields: 16 squares | **Prep Time:** 10 minutes | **Inactive Time:** overnight

INGREDIENTS

For the peanut butter:
1 cup peanut butter
½ cup coconut flour
½ cup maple syrup
½ teaspoon vanilla extract

For the chia seed jam layer:
2 cups strawberries
½ cup medjool dates, pitted
¼ cup chia seeds
1 tablespoon coconut oil

tip: You can use other fruits for the chia seed jam, like raspberries or dark sweet cherries!

DIRECTIONS

Prepare the peanut butter layer:

1. Prepare an 8 × 8 baking dish lined with parchment paper. Set aside.

2. Add all ingredients for the peanut butter layer to a medium-sized bowl and stir until everything is well combined.

3. Transfer the mixture into the prepared baking dish and spread it evenly on the bottom of the dish. Set aside.

Prepare the chia seed jam layer:

1. Add all ingredients for the chia seed jam layer to a food processor and process until the dates are broken down into small pieces and everything is well combined.

2. Transfer the chia seed jam layer to the baking dish and spread it evenly over the top of the peanut butter layer.

(continued on next page)

3. Using the tip of a sharp knife, swirl the chia seed jam mixture into the peanut butter layer, then spread it evenly over the top.

Assembly:

1. Place the baking dish in the freezer overnight, or until the squares are firm.

2. Remove the baking dish from the freezer and cut into 16 squares.

3. Store in an air-tight container in the freezer or refrigerator until ready to serve, because the squares will get soft if left out at room temperature.

TRIPLE CHOCOLATE ALMOND BUTTER SQUARES

Yields: 8 large squares | **Prep Time:** 10 minutes | **Inactive Time:** 60 minutes

INGREDIENTS

For the chocolate crust layer:
2 cups brown rice crisps cereal
½ cup almond butter
½ cup cacao powder
¼ cup maple syrup
2 tablespoons coconut oil
1 teaspoon vanilla extract
⅛ teaspoon sea salt

For the chocolate almond butter layer:
1 cup almond butter
¼ cup cacao powder
2 tablespoons maple syrup
2 tablespoons coconut oil
⅛ teaspoon sea salt

For the chocolate drizzle:
¼ cup semi-sweet mini chocolate chips
½ teaspoon coconut oil

tip: In the mood for chocolate and peanut butter? Substitute the almond butter in the recipe for peanut butter!

DIRECTIONS

Prepare the chocolate crust layer:

1. Prepare a 9 × 5 loaf pan lined with parchment paper. Set aside.

2. Add all ingredients for the crust layer to a food processor and process until everything is well combined, taking care to not over process.

3. Transfer the mixture into the prepared loaf pan and spread it evenly on the bottom of the pan. Place an extra piece of parchment paper on top of the chocolate crust mixture and press it down very tight and compact. Set aside.

Prepare the chocolate almond butter layer:

1. Add all ingredients for the chocolate almond butter layer to a medium-sized bowl and stir until everything is well combined.

(continued on next page)

2. Transfer the chocolate almond butter layer to the baking dish and spread it evenly over the top of the chocolate crust layer.

Prepare the chocolate drizzle:

1. Add all ingredients for the chocolate drizzle to a small saucepan and melt on lowest heat, stirring until it is completely melted and smooth, taking care to not let it burn.

2. Using a spoon, drizzle the melted chocolate evenly over the top of the chocolate almond butter layer.

Assembly:

1. Place the loaf pan in the freezer for approximately 60 minutes, or until the squares are firm.

2. Remove the loaf pan from the freezer and cut into 8 large squares.

3. Store in an air-tight container in the freezer or refrigerator until ready to serve, because the squares will get soft if left out at room temperature.

5

cheesecakes, tarts + ice cream

CHOCOLATE PEANUT BUTTER CHEESECAKE

Yields: 8 small slices | **Prep Time:** 15 minutes | **Inactive Time:** 1 hour + overnight

INGREDIENTS

For the crust:
1 cup pecans
½ cup medjool dates, pitted
2 tablespoons cacao powder
1 tablespoon coconut oil
½ teaspoon vanilla extract
⅛ teaspoon sea salt

For the cheesecake filling:
3 cups cashews, soaked for 1 hour and
    drained*
1 can full-fat coconut milk, 13.5-ounce can
½ cup peanut butter
¾ cup maple syrup
¼ cup coconut oil
¼ cup cacao powder

For the chocolate peanut butter topping:
1 cup semi-sweet mini chocolate chips
½ cup peanut butter

For the peanut butter balls garnish:
2 tablespoons cacao powder
½ cup peanut butter
1–2 teaspoons coconut flour, if needed

DIRECTIONS

Prepare the crust:

1. Set aside a 6-inch springform cheesecake pan.

2. Add all ingredients for the crust to a food processor and process until the pecans and dates are broken down into small pieces and everything is well combined, taking care to not over process.

3. Transfer the mixture into the cheesecake pan and spread it evenly on the bottom of the pan. Place a piece of parchment paper on top of the crust mixture and press it down very tight and compact. Set aside.

Prepare the cheesecake filling:

1. Add all ingredients for the cheesecake filling to a food processor and process until the cashews are completely broken down and everything is creamy and smooth. This should take approximately

(continued on next page)

5 minutes, and you may have to stop and scrape the sides several times to help it along.

2. Transfer the cheesecake filling to the cheesecake pan and spread it evenly over the top of the crust layer.

3. Gently tap the cheesecake pan on the countertop so the cheesecake mixture settles.

4. Transfer the cheesecake pan to the freezer for approximately 30 minutes, to firm while you prepare the other steps.

Prepare the peanut butter balls garnish:

1. Add the cacao powder to a small bowl. Set aside.

2. Add the peanut butter to another small bowl. Depending on the consistency of the peanut butter, you many need to add coconut flour until the peanut butter is firm enough to roll into a ball shape. Add 1 teaspoon of coconut flour at a time until it firms, but only as needed.

3. Take about ½ tablespoon of the peanut butter at a time, squeeze it tightly in your fist to make it compact, then roll it between the palms of your hands into a small ball shape.

4. Toss each ball in the small bowl of cacao powder garnish until they are completely covered. Set aside.

Prepare the chocolate peanut butter topping:

1. Add all ingredients for the chocolate peanut butter topping to a small saucepan and melt on lowest heat, stirring until it is completely melted and smooth, taking care to not let it burn.

Assembly:

1. Remove the cheesecake pan from the freezer. Pour the chocolate peanut butter topping mixture evenly over the top of the cheesecake filling.

2. Gently place the peanut butter ball garnish onto the chocolate peanut butter topping around the outer top edge of the cheesecake.

3. Place the cheesecake pan in the freezer overnight, or until firm.

4. Remove from the freezer when ready to serve, gently release the cheesecake from the cheesecake pan, and cut into 8 small slices.

5. Store in an air-tight container in the freezer or refrigerator until ready to serve, because the cheesecake will get soft if left out at room temperature.

tip: *To make sure the cheesecake filling is as smooth and creamy as possible, you will need to soak the cashews for at least 1 hour in a bowl of water, then drain and rinse before adding them to the food processor.

KIWI + COCONUT CHEESECAKE SQUARES

Yields: 16 squares | **Prep Time:** 10 minutes | **Inactive Time:** 1 hour + overnight

INGREDIENTS

For the crust:

2 cup pecans
1 cup medjool dates, pitted
½ cup unsweetened shredded coconut
2 tablespoons coconut oil
1 teaspoon vanilla extract
⅛ teaspoon sea salt

For the cheesecake filling:

3 cups cashews, soaked for 1 hour and
    drained*
½ cup maple syrup
4 kiwi, peeled and quartered
¼ cup lemon juice
¼ cup coconut oil
⅛ teaspoon sea salt

For the garnish:

½ cup unsweetened shredded coconut
2–3 kiwi, peeled and sliced

DIRECTIONS

Prepare the crust:

1. Prepare an 8 × 8 baking dish lined with parchment paper. Set aside.

2. Add all ingredients for the crust to a food processor and process until the pecans and dates are broken down into small pieces and everything is well combined, taking care to not over process.

3. Transfer the mixture into the prepared baking dish and spread it evenly on the bottom of the dish. Place an extra piece of parchment paper on top of the crust mixture and press it down very tight and compact. Set aside.

Prepare the cheesecake filling:

1. Add all ingredients for the cheesecake filling to a food processor and process until the cashews are completely broken down and everything is creamy and smooth. This should take approximately

(continued on next page)

5 minutes, and you may have to stop and scrape the sides several times to help it along.

2. Transfer the cheesecake filling to the baking dish and spread it evenly over the top of the crust.

3. Gently tap the cheesecake pan on the countertop so the cheesecake filling settles.

4. Sprinkle the shredded coconut garnish evenly over the top of the cheesecake filling and gently pat it down so it's slightly embedded into the cheesecake filling.

Assembly:

1. Place the baking dish in the freezer overnight, or until firm.

2. Remove from the freezer and cut into 16 squares.

3. Garnish the top of each square with a slice of kiwi.

4. Store in an air-tight container in the freezer or refrigerator until ready to serve, because the squares will get soft if left out at room temperature.

tip: *To make sure the cheesecake filling is as smooth and creamy as possible, you will need to soak the cashews for at least 1 hour in a bowl of water, then drain and rinse before adding them to the food processor.

MANGO CHOCOLATE CHIP CHEESECAKE

Yields: 8 small slices | **Prep Time:** 10 minutes | **Inactive Time:** 1 hour + overnight

INGREDIENTS

For the crust:
1 cup pecans
½ cup medjool dates, pitted
1 tablespoon cacao powder
1 tablespoon coconut oil
½ teaspoon vanilla extract

For the cheesecake filling:
1½ cups cashews, soaked for 1 hour and
    drained*
1 cup mango, peeled and cubed
¼ cup maple syrup
2 tablespoons coconut oil
2 tablespoons water

For the add-in:
1 cup semi-sweet mini chocolate chips

For the garnish:
½ cup semi-sweet mini chocolate chips

DIRECTIONS

Prepare the crust:

1. Set aside a 6-inch springform cheesecake pan.

2. Add all ingredients for the crust to a food processor and process until the pecans and dates are broken down into small pieces and everything is well combined, taking care to not over process.

3. Transfer the mixture into the cheesecake pan and spread it evenly on the bottom of the pan. Place a piece of parchment paper on top of the crust mixture and press it down very tight and compact. Set aside.

Prepare the cheesecake filling:

1. Add all ingredients for the cheesecake filling to a food processor and process until the cashews are completely broken down and everything is creamy and smooth. This should take approximately

(continued on next page)

5 minutes, and you may have to stop and scrape the sides several times to help it along.

2. Add the chocolate chip add-in to the food processor and stir in by hand until it is evenly distributed.

3. Transfer the cheesecake filling to the cheesecake pan and spread it evenly over the top of the crust.

4. Gently tap the cheesecake pan on the countertop so the cheesecake filling settles.

5. Sprinkle the chocolate chip garnish evenly over the top of the cheesecake filling and gently pat it down so it's slightly embedded into the cheesecake filling.

Assembly:

1. Place the cheesecake pan in the freezer overnight, or until firm.

2. Remove from the freezer when ready to serve, gently release the cheesecake from the cheesecake pan, and cut into 8 small slices.

3. Store in an air-tight container in the freezer or refrigerator until ready to serve, because the cheesecake will get soft if left out at room temperature.

tip: *To make sure the cheesecake filling is as smooth and creamy as possible, you will need to soak the cashews for at least 1 hour in a bowl of water, then drain and rinse before adding them to the food processor.

tip: You can make this dessert all year round even if fresh mango isn't in season—just use frozen diced mango!

CHOCOLATE FUDGE TARTS

Yields: 2 individual 4-inch tarts | **Prep Time:** 10 minutes | **Inactive Time:** 60 minutes

INGREDIENTS

For the crust:
½ cup walnuts
1 cup medjool dates, pitted
2 tablespoons cacao powder
1 tablespoon coconut oil

For the chocolate fudge filling:
½ cup almond butter
½ cup coconut oil
½ cup maple syrup
¼ cup cacao powder
⅛ teaspoon sea salt

For the garnish:
¼ cup freeze-dried raspberries

DIRECTIONS

Prepare the crust:

1. Set aside 2 individual 4-inch tart pans.

2. Add all ingredients for the crust to a food processor and process until the walnuts and dates are broken down into small pieces and everything is well combined, taking care to not over process.

3. Divide the crust mixture evenly between the two tart pans, pressing it down so it is very tight and compact. Set aside.

Prepare the chocolate fudge filling:

1. Add all ingredients for the chocolate fudge filling to a medium-sized bowl and stir until everything is well combined and smooth.

2. Divide the chocolate fudge filling evenly between the 2 tart pans and pour it on top of the crusts.

3. Gently tap the tart pans on the countertop so the filling settles.

Assembly:

1. Place the tart pans in the freezer for approximately 60 minutes, or until firm.

2. Remove from the freezer when ready to serve, gently release the tarts from the tart pan, and cut into 4 small slices per tart pan.

3. Sprinkle the freeze-dried raspberry garnish over the top of the tarts.

4. Store in an air-tight container in the freezer or refrigerator until ready to serve, because the tarts will get soft if left out at room temperature.

BLUEBERRY LEMON TARTS WITH ALMOND CRUST

Yields: 2 individual 4-inch tarts | **Prep Time:** 10 minutes | **Inactive Time:** 1 hour + 60 minutes

INGREDIENTS

For the crust:
1 cup almonds
1 cup medjool dates, pitted
2 tablespoons coconut oil

For the filling:
2 cups cashews, soaked for 1 hour and drained*
¼ cup maple syrup
¼ cup lemon juice
1 teaspoon vanilla extract
⅛ teaspoon sea salt

For the garnish:
1 cup blueberries

DIRECTIONS

Prepare the crust:

1. Set aside 2 individual 4-inch tart pans.

2. Add all ingredients for the crust to a food processor and process until the almonds and dates are broken down into small pieces and everything is well combined, taking care to not over process.

3. Divide the mixture evenly between the two tart pans, pressing it down so it is very tight and compact. Set aside.

Prepare the filling:

1. Add all ingredients for the filling to a food processor and process until the cashews are completely broken down and everything is creamy and smooth. This should take approximately 5 minutes, and you may have to stop and scrape the sides several times to help it along.

2. Divide the filling evenly between the 2 tart pans and pour it on top of the crusts.

(continued on next page)

3. Gently tap the tart pans on the countertop so the filling settles.

4. Divide the blueberry garnish evenly between the two tart pans, adding it on top of the filling.

Assembly:

1. Place the tart pans in the refrigerator for approximately 60 minutes, or until firm.

2. Remove from the refrigerator when ready to serve, gently release the tarts from the tart pan, and cut into 4 small slices per tart pan.

3. Store in an air-tight container in the refrigerator until ready to serve, because they will get soft if left out at room temperature.

tip: *To make sure the cheesecake filling is as smooth and creamy as possible, you will need to soak the cashews for at least 1 hour in a bowl of water, then drain and rinse before adding them to the food processor.

tip: Change it up by using a different berry like raspberries or blackberries, which also pair well with lemon!

PISTACHIO + CHOCOLATE MINI CHEESECAKES

Yields: 12 mini cheesecakes | **Prep Time:** 10 minutes | **Inactive Time:** 1 hour + overnight

INGREDIENTS

For the crust:
2 cup pecans
1 cup medjool dates, pitted
¼ cup cacao powder
¼ cup coconut oil

For the cheesecake filling:
2 cups cashews, soaked for 1 hour and
    drained*
½ cup maple syrup
½ cup pistachios
6 tablespoons coconut oil
2 tablespoons lemon juice
1 teaspoon vanilla extract

For the garnish:
½ cup pistachios, chopped

DIRECTIONS

Prepare the crust:

1. Set aside a 12-cavity mini cheesecake pan.

2. Add all ingredients for the crust to a food processor and process until the pecans and dates are broken down into small pieces and everything is well combined, taking care to not over process.

3. Transfer the mixture to the mini cheesecake pan and divide it equally between the 12 cavities, pressing it down so it is very tight and compact. Set aside.

Prepare the cheesecake filling:

1. Add all ingredients for the cheesecake filling to a food processor and process until the cashews are completely broken down and everything is creamy and smooth. This should take approximately 5 minutes, and you may have to stop and scrape the sides several times to help it along.

(continued on next page)

2. Pour the cheesecake filling on top of each crust, dividing it equally between the 12 cavities.

3. Gently tap the cheesecake pan on the countertop so the cheesecake filling settles.

4. Sprinkle the chopped pistachio garnish over the top of each cheesecake.

Assembly:

1. Place the cheesecake pan in the freezer overnight, or until firm.

2. Remove from the freezer when ready to serve, and gently release the cheesecakes from the cheesecake pan.

3. Store in an air-tight container in the freezer or refrigerator until ready to serve, because they will get soft if left out at room temperature.

tip: *To make sure the cheesecake filling is as smooth and creamy as possible, you will need to soak the cashews for at least 1 hour in a bowl of water, then drain and rinse before adding them to the food processor.

tip: You can make these without a mini cheesecake pan—just divide the crust and cheesecake mixture evenly between 12 standard-size muffin cups!

CARAMEL + CHOCOLATE TARTS

Yields: 4 individual 4-inch tarts | Prep Time: 15 minutes | Inactive Time: 60 minutes

INGREDIENTS

For the crust:
1 cup almonds
1 cup medjool dates, pitted
2 tablespoons cacao powder
1 tablespoon coconut oil

For the caramel filling:
1¼ cup medjool dates, pitted
2½ tablespoons almond butter
1¼ teaspoon vanilla extract
¼ teaspoon sea salt

DIRECTIONS

Prepare the crust:

1. Set aside 4 individual 4-inch tart pans.

2. Add all ingredients for the crust to a food processor and process until the almonds and dates are broken down into small pieces and everything is well combined, taking care to not over process.

3. Divide the mixture evenly between the four tart pans, pressing it down so it is very tight and compact. Set aside.

Prepare the caramel filling:

1. Add all ingredients for the caramel filling to a food processor and process until the dates are broken down and everything is well combined.

2. Divide the filling evenly between the 4 tart pans and spread it evenly over the top of the crusts.

Assembly:

1. Place the tart pans in the freezer for approximately 60 minutes, or until firm.

2. Remove from the freezer when ready to serve, gently release the tarts from the tart pan, and cut into 4 small slices per tart pan.

3. Store in an air-tight container in the freezer or refrigerator until ready to serve, because the tarts will get soft if left out at room temperature.

PUMPKIN PIE TARTS

Yields: 4 individual 4-inch tarts | **Prep Time:** 10 minutes | **Inactive Time:** 60 minutes

INGREDIENTS

For the crust:
2 cups pecans
1 cup medjool dates, pitted
¼ cup coconut oil
1 teaspoon vanilla extract
½ teaspoon pumpkin spice
¼ teaspoon sea salt

For the pumpkin filling:
1 can pumpkin puree, 15-ounce can
½ cup medjool dates, pitted
¼ cup coconut oil
2 tablespoons maple syrup
2 teaspoons vanilla extract
1 teaspoon pumpkin spice
⅛ teaspoon sea salt

DIRECTIONS

Prepare the crust:

1. Set aside 4 individual 4-inch tart pans.

2. Add all ingredients for the crust to a food processor and process until the pecans and dates are broken down into small pieces and everything is well combined, taking care to not over process.

3. Divide the crust evenly between the 4 tart pans, pressing it down very tight and compact. Set aside.

Prepare the pumpkin filling:

1. Add all ingredients for the pumpkin filling to a food processor and process until the dates are broken down into small pieces and everything is well combined.

2. Divide the pumpkin filling evenly between the 4 tart pans and spread it evenly over the top of the crust.

Assembly:

1. Place the tart pans in the freezer for approximately 60 minutes, or until firm.

2. Remove from the freezer when ready to serve, gently release the tarts from the tart pan, and cut into 4 small slices per tart pan.

3. Store in an air-tight container in the freezer or refrigerator until ready to serve, because the tarts will get soft if left out at room temperature.

CHOCOLATE "NICE" CREAM

Yields: 4 small servings | **Prep Time:** 5 minutes | **Inactive Time:** overnight

INGREDIENTS

4 bananas, ripe and frozen
2 tablespoons cacao powder
2 tablespoons almond butter
1 tablespoon maple syrup
1 teaspoon vanilla extract

tip: I chose a classic chocolate flavor in this recipe, but you can use the frozen bananas as a base for unlimited "nice" cream flavor possibilities. Add your favorite fruit like raspberries, blueberries, mango, or other add-ins like peanut butter or chocolate chips!

DIRECTIONS

1. Break the frozen bananas into small pieces and add with the remaining ingredients to a food processor. Process until the bananas are completely broken down and everything is creamy and smooth, taking care to not over process. It should have the consistency of soft-serve ice cream. This should take approximately 1 to 2 minutes and you may have to stop and scrape the sides several times to help it along.

2. Serve immediately or store in an air-tight container in the freezer because the "nice" cream will get soft if left out at room temperature.

PECAN PRALINE ICE CREAM

Yields: 4 servings | **Prep Time:** 10 minutes | **Inactive Time:** overnight

INGREDIENTS

For the ice cream:
1 can full-fat coconut milk, 13.5-ounce can
¼ cup coconut sugar
1 teaspoon vanilla extract

For the praline:
1 cup medjool dates, pitted
¼ cup water
1 teaspoon vanilla extract

For the add-in:
1 cup pecans

DIRECTIONS

Prepare the ice cream:

1. Set aside a 9 × 5 loaf pan.

2. Add all ingredients for the ice cream to a medium-sized bowl and whisk until everything is well combined and smooth. If you have a blender, you can also mix the ice cream mixture in your blender.

3. Transfer the ice cream mixture into the loaf pan. Set aside.

Prepare the praline:

1. Add all ingredients for the praline to a food processor and process until the dates are broken down into small pieces and everything is well combined.

2. Take out a handful at a time and sprinkle it evenly into the ice cream mixture.

3. Sprinkle the pecan add-in evenly over the top of the ice cream mixture and gently pat it down so it's slightly embedded into the ice cream mixture.

Assembly:

1. Tightly cover the loaf pan and place in the freezer overnight, or until the ice cream is firm.

2. Store in an air-tight container in the freezer until ready to serve because the ice cream will get soft if left out at room temperature.

PISTACHIO AVOCADO ICE CREAM

Yields: 4 servings | **Prep Time:** 10 minutes | **Inactive Time:** 30 minutes

INGREDIENTS

For the pistachio nut butter:
1 cup pistachios

For the ice cream:
2 avocados
¼ cup maple syrup
1 teaspoon vanilla extract

tip: Want to add some chocolate? Stir in mini-chocolate chips to the ice cream mixture before putting in the freezer, or drizzle melted chocolate over the ice cream before serving!

DIRECTIONS

Prepare the pistachio nut butter:

1. Add the pistachios to a food processor and process until they are broken down into a thick and creamy nut butter. This will take approximately 5 minutes, and you may need to stop one or two times to scrape the sides and help it along. Set aside.

Prepare the ice cream:

1. Set aside a 9 × 5 loaf pan.

2. Add all ingredients for the ice cream to the food processor with the pistachio nut butter, and process until everything is well combined and smooth.

3. Pour the ice cream mixture evenly into the loaf pan.

Assembly:

1. Tightly cover the loaf pan and place in the freezer overnight, or until the ice cream is firm.

2. Store in an air-tight container in the freezer until ready to serve because the ice cream will get soft if left out at room temperature.

PEANUT BUTTER BROWNIE ICE CREAM

Yields: 4 servings | **Prep Time:** 10 minutes | **Inactive Time:** 1 hour + overnight

INGREDIENTS

For the ice cream:
1 cup cashews, soaked for 1 hour and
    drained*
1 can full-fat coconut milk, 13.5-ounce can
½ cup peanut butter
½ cup coconut sugar
1 teaspoon vanilla extract
¼ teaspoon sea salt

For the brownie add-in:
1 cup medjool dates, pitted
½ cup cacao powder
½ cup sunflower seeds
½ cup hemp seeds
2 tablespoons coconut oil
1 teaspoon vanilla extract
⅛ teaspoon sea salt

tip: *To make sure the cheesecake filling is as smooth and creamy as possible, you will need to soak the cashews for at least 1 hour in a bowl of water, then drain and rinse before adding them to the food processor.

DIRECTIONS

Prepare the ice cream:

1. Set aside a 9 × 5 loaf pan.

2. Add all ingredients for the ice cream to a food processor and process until the cashews are completely broken down and everything is creamy and smooth. This should take approximately 5 minutes, and you may have to stop and scrape the sides several times to help it along.

3. Transfer the ice cream mixture into the loaf pan. Set aside.

Prepare the brownie add-in:

1. Add all ingredients for the brownie add-in to a food processor and process until the seeds and dates are broken down into small pieces and everything is well combined, taking care to not over process.

2. Sprinkle a handful at a time evenly over the top of the ice cream mixture, and using a fork, gently pat the brownie pieces into the ice cream mixture.

(continued on next page)

Assembly:

1. Tightly cover the loaf pan and place in the freezer overnight, or until the ice cream is firm.

2. Store in an air-tight container in the freezer until ready to serve because the ice cream will get soft if left out at room temperature.

6

candy bars + classics

PEANUT BUTTER CUPS

Yields: 8 pieces | **Prep Time:** 10 minutes | **Inactive Time:** 60 minutes

INGREDIENTS

For the peanut butter filling:
1 cup peanut butter
¼ cup maple syrup
¼ cup coconut oil

For the chocolate coating:
1 cup semi-sweet mini chocolate chips
1 tablespoon coconut oil

DIRECTIONS

Prep directions:

1. Prepare a cookie sheet with 8 standard-size muffin cups on top. Place the cookie sheet in the freezer to chill while you prepare the other steps.

Prepare the peanut butter filling:

1. Add all ingredients for the peanut butter filling to a medium-sized bowl and stir until everything is well combined and smooth. Set aside.

Prepare the chocolate coating:

1. Add all ingredients for the chocolate coating to a small saucepan and melt on lowest heat, stirring until it is completely melted and smooth, taking care to not let it burn.

Assembly:

1. Remove the cookie sheet from the freezer. Take a spoonful at a time of the chocolate coating and place into the bottom of each muffin cup.

2. Holding the bottom of the muffin cup with one hand and slowly turning clockwise, use a spoon with the other hand to gently spread the chocolate coating from the bottom of the cup up along the sides of the cup.

3. Place the cookie sheet in the freezer for approximately 5 minutes, or until the chocolate hardens.

4. Remove the cookie sheet from the freezer. Take a spoonful at a time of the peanut butter filling and place into the center of each muffin cup.

5. Gently tap each muffin cup on the countertop so the peanut butter filling settles.

(continued on next page)

6. Divide the remaining chocolate coating evenly between the 8 muffin cups, adding it on top of the peanut butter filling.

7. Place the cookie sheet in the freezer for approximately 60 minutes, or until the chocolate hardens.

8. Store in an air-tight container in the freezer or refrigerator until ready to serve, because they will get soft if left out at room temperature.

tip: You can make mini-peanut butter cups, too! Just divide the peanut butter filling and chocolate coating evenly between mini-muffin cups for a bite-sized treat.

TWIX BARS

Yields: 7 full-size bars or 14 mini bars | **Prep Time:** 15 minutes | **Inactive Time:** 60 minutes

INGREDIENTS

For the cookie layer:
1 cup almond flour
¼ cup maple syrup
¼ cup coconut oil
1 tablespoon coconut flour
½ teaspoon vanilla extract
⅛ teaspoon sea salt

For the caramel layer:
1 cup medjool dates, pitted
1 tablespoon peanut butter
1 tablespoon coconut oil
1 teaspoon vanilla extract
⅛ teaspoon sea salt

For the chocolate coating:
1 cup semi-sweet mini chocolate chips
1 tablespoon peanut butter
1 tablespoon coconut oil

DIRECTIONS

Prepare the cookie layer:

1. Prepare a 9 × 5 loaf pan lined with parchment paper. Set aside.

2. Add all ingredients for the cookie layer to a medium-sized bowl and stir until everything is well combined.

3. Transfer the mixture into the prepared loaf pan and spread it evenly on the bottom of the pan. Place an extra piece of parchment paper on top of the cookie mixture and press it down very tight and compact.

4. Transfer the loaf pan to the freezer for approximately 15 minutes, or until firm.

Prepare the caramel layer:

1. Add all ingredients for the caramel layer to a food processor and process until the dates are broken down into small pieces and everything is well combined, taking care to not over process.

2. Remove the loaf pan from the freezer and transfer the caramel layer mixture into the loaf pan, spreading it evenly over the top of the cookie layer.

(continued on next page)

3. Transfer the loaf pan back to the freezer for approximately 15 minutes, or until firm.

Prepare the chocolate coating:

1. Add all ingredients for the chocolate coating to a small saucepan and melt on lowest heat, stirring until it is completely melted and smooth, taking care to not let it burn. Set aside.

Assembly:

1. Prepare a cookie sheet lined with parchment paper. Set aside.

2. Remove the loaf pan from the freezer and cut into 7 full-size bars or 14 mini bars.

3. Dip each bar into the chocolate coating until the bars are completely covered on all sides; use a fork to flip them over and to allow the excess chocolate to drip off.

4. Place the bars onto the prepared cookie sheet and return to the freezer for approximately 30 minutes, or until the chocolate hardens.

5. Store in an air-tight container in the freezer or refrigerator until ready to serve, because the bars will get soft if left out at room temperature.

ALMOND JOY BARS

Yields: 7 full-size bars or 14 mini bars | **Prep Time:** 15 minutes | **Inactive Time:** 90 minutes

INGREDIENTS

For the bars:
2½ cups unsweetened shredded coconut
¼ cup coconut oil
¼ cup maple syrup
1 teaspoon vanilla extract
⅛ teaspoon sea salt

For the add-in:
½ cup almonds, 56 pieces

For the chocolate coating:
1 cup semi-sweet mini chocolate chips
1 tablespoon coconut oil

DIRECTIONS

Prepare the bars:

1. Prepare a 9 × 5 loaf pan lined with parchment paper. Set aside.

2. Add all ingredients for the bars to a food processor and process until everything is well combined.

3. Transfer the mixture into the prepared loaf pan and spread it evenly on the bottom of the pan. Place an extra piece of parchment paper on top of the bar mixture and press it down very tight and compact.

4. Add the almond add-ins to the top of the bars, placing them side-by-side until they completely cover the top of the bars in 4 rows with 14 almonds in each row. (When you cut the bars vertically into 7 slices, each bar should have 2 vertical rows of almonds on each one, or 8 almonds per bar.)

5. Press the almonds down so they are slightly embedded into the bar mixture.

6. Transfer the loaf pan to the freezer for approximately 60 minutes, or until the bars are firm.

Prepare the chocolate coating:

1. After the bars have firmed in the freezer, add all ingredients for the chocolate coating to a small saucepan and melt on lowest heat, stirring until it is completely melted and smooth, taking care to not let it burn. Set aside.

Assembly:

1. Prepare a cookie sheet lined with parchment paper. Set aside.

(continued on next page)

2. Remove the loaf pan from the freezer and cut into 7 full-size bars or 14 mini bars.

3. Dip each bar into the chocolate coating until the bars are completely covered on all sides; use a fork to flip them over and to allow the excess chocolate to drip off.

4. Place the bars onto the prepared cookie sheet and return to the freezer for approximately 30 minutes, or until the chocolate hardens.

5. Store in an air-tight container in the freezer or refrigerator until ready to serve, because the bars will get soft if left out at room temperature.

SNICKERS BARS

Yields: 6 full-size bars or 12 mini bars | **Prep Time:** 15 minutes | **Inactive Time:** 30 minutes

INGREDIENTS

For the nougat layer:
1 cup gluten-free quick rolled oats
½ cup medjool dates, pitted
2 tablespoons peanut butter
1 tablespoon coconut oil
¼ teaspoon vanilla extract
⅛ teaspoon sea salt

For the caramel layer:
1 cup medjool dates, pitted
2 tablespoons peanut butter
1 teaspoon vanilla extract
¼ teaspoon sea salt

For the peanut layer:
½ cup peanuts

For the chocolate coating:
1 cup semi-sweet mini chocolate chips
1 tablespoon coconut oil

DIRECTIONS

Prepare the nougat layer:

1. Prepare a 9 × 5 loaf pan lined with parchment paper. Set aside.

2. Add all ingredients for the nougat layer to a food processor and process until the dates are broken down into small pieces and the oats are as fine as possible.

3. Transfer the mixture into the prepared loaf pan and spread it evenly on the bottom of the pan. Place an extra piece of parchment paper on top of the nougat mixture and press it down very tight and compact. Set aside.

Prepare the caramel layer:

1. Add all ingredients for the caramel layer to a food processor and process until the dates are broken down into small pieces and everything is well combined, taking care to not over process.

2. Transfer the mixture to the loaf pan and spread it evenly over the top of the nougat layer.

(continued on next page)

Prepare the peanut layer:

1. Sprinkle the peanuts for the peanut layer evenly over the top of the caramel layer and gently pat them down so they are slightly embedded into the caramel layer.

2. Place the loaf pan in the freezer for approximately 30 minutes, or until the bars are firm.

Prepare the chocolate coating:

1. After the bars have firmed in the freezer, add all ingredients for the chocolate coating to a small saucepan and melt on lowest heat, stirring until it is completely melted and smooth, taking care to not let it burn. Set aside.

Assembly:

1. Prepare a cookie sheet lined with parchment paper. Set aside.

2. Remove the loaf pan from the freezer and cut into 6 full-size bars or 12 mini bars.

3. Dip each bar into the chocolate coating until the bar is completely covered on all sides; use a fork to flip them over and to allow the excess chocolate to drip off.

4. Place the bars onto the prepared cookie sheet and return to the freezer for approximately 30 minutes, or until the chocolate hardens.

5. Store in an air-tight container in the freezer or refrigerator until ready to serve, because the bars will get soft if left out at room temperature.

CHOCOLATE CRUNCH BITES

Yields: 10 pieces | **Prep Time:** 10 minutes | **Inactive Time:** 30 minutes

INGREDIENTS

For the chocolate:
1 cup semi-sweet mini chocolate chips
1 tablespoon coconut oil
1 teaspoon vanilla extract
⅛ teaspoon sea salt

For the add-in:
2 cups brown rice crisps cereal

DIRECTIONS

1. Prepare a cookie sheet and place a candy mold of your choice on top (ice cube tray, silicone candy bar mold, mini muffin cups, etc.). Set aside.

2. Add all ingredients for the chocolate to a small saucepan and melt on lowest heat, stirring until it is completely melted and smooth, taking care to not let it burn. Transfer the chocolate to a medium-sized bowl.

3. Add the brown rice crisps cereal add-in and stir in by hand until they are evenly distributed.

4. Take one spoonful at a time and place it into the mold of your choice, spreading it evenly on the bottom of the mold and pressing it down so it is very tight and compact.

5. Place the cookie sheet in the freezer for approximately 30 minutes, or until the chocolate hardens.

6. Store in an air-tight container in the freezer until ready to serve, because they will get soft if left out at room temperature.

CRISPY TREAT SQUARES

Yields: 16 squares | **Prep Time:** 10 minutes | **Inactive Time:** 60 minutes

INGREDIENTS

For the squares:
1 cup medjool dates, pitted
½ cup cashew butter
¼ cup coconut oil
2 tablespoons maple syrup
2 teaspoons vanilla extract
⅛ teaspoon sea salt

For the add-in:
4 cups brown rice crisps cereal

DIRECTIONS

1. Prepare an 8 × 8 baking dish lined with parchment paper. Set aside.

2. Add all ingredients for the squares to a food processor and process until the dates are broken down into small pieces and everything is well combined, taking care to not over process.

3. Transfer the mixture to a large mixing bowl. Add the brown rice crisps cereal add-in and stir by hand until they are evenly distributed.

4. Transfer the mixture into the prepared baking dish and spread it evenly on the bottom of the dish. Place an extra piece of parchment paper on top of the mixture and press it down very tight and compact.

5. Place the baking dish in the freezer for approximately 60 minutes, or until the squares are firm.

6. Remove the baking dish from the freezer and cut into 16 squares.

7. Store in an air-tight container in the freezer or refrigerator until ready to serve, because the squares will get soft if let out at room temperature.

tip: Love peanut butter? You can substitute peanut butter for the cashew butter for a fun twist!

BUCKEYES

Yields: 14 pieces | **Prep Time:** 10 minutes | **Inactive Time:** 60 minutes

INGREDIENTS

For the peanut butter balls:
1 cup peanut butter
½ cup + 2 tablespoons coconut flour
¼ cup maple syrup
1 teaspoon vanilla extract
1–2 teaspoons coconut flour, if needed

For the chocolate coating:
½ cup semi-sweet mini chocolate chips
1 tablespoon peanut butter
1 teaspoon coconut oil

DIRECTIONS

Prepare the peanut butter balls:

1. Prepare a cookie sheet lined with parchment paper. Set aside.

2. Add all ingredients for the peanut butter balls to a medium-sized bowl and stir until everything is well combined and smooth. Depending on the consistency of the peanut butter, you may need to add extra coconut flour until the mixture is firm enough to roll into a ball shape. Add 1 teaspoon at a time until it firms, but only as needed.

3. Take one handful of the mixture at a time and roll it between the palms of your hands into a ball shape.

4. Place the balls onto the prepared cookie sheet.

5. Transfer the cookie sheet to the freezer for approximately 30 minutes, or until the balls are firm.

Prepare the chocolate coating:

1. Add all ingredients for the chocolate coating to a small saucepan and melt on lowest heat until it's completely melted and smooth, taking care to not let it burn.

Assembly:

1. Remove the cookie sheet from the freezer.

2. Using a toothpick or the tip of a fork, dip each ball into the chocolate coating, leaving the top part of the ball exposed. Use your fingertips to smooth out the toothpick or fork holes if you prefer the tops to be smooth.

3. Place the balls back onto the cookie sheet. Return the cookie sheet to the freezer for approximately 30 minutes, or until the chocolate hardens.

4. Store in an air-tight container in the freezer or refrigerator until ready to serve, because they will get soft if left out at room temperature.

tip: Leaving the top part of the peanut butter ball exposed gives this recipe the classic "buckeye" look, but you can skip that step and dip the entire ball into the melted chocolate if you like!

PEANUT BUTTER TAG-A-LONGS

Yields: 10 cookies | **Prep Time:** 15 minutes | **Inactive Time:** 60 minutes

INGREDIENTS

For the cookie layer:
1 cup almond flour
¼ cup maple syrup
¼ cup coconut oil
2 tablespoons coconut flour
¼ teaspoon vanilla extract
⅛ teaspoon sea salt

For the peanut butter filling:
¾ cup peanut butter
2 tablespoons maple syrup
2 tablespoons coconut flour
1–2 tablespoons coconut flour, if needed

For the chocolate coating:
1 cup semi-sweet mini chocolate chips
1 tablespoon coconut oil

DIRECTIONS

Prepare the cookie layer:

1. Prepare a cookie sheet lined with parchment paper. Set aside.

2. Add all ingredients for the cookie layer to a medium-sized bowl and stir until everything is well combined.

3. Transfer the mixture onto the prepared cookie sheet. Place an extra piece of parchment paper on top of the cookie mixture and press it down evenly into a flat 8 × 8 square shape.

4. Place the cookie sheet in the freezer for approximately 15 minutes, or until the cookie layer is firm.

Prepare the peanut butter filling:

1. Add all ingredients for the peanut butter filling to a small bowl and stir until everything is well combined and smooth. Depending on the type of peanut butter you use, you may have to add 1 to 2 extra tablespoons of coconut flour to get the mixture thick enough to roll it into a ball shape. Add 1 tablespoon of flour at a time until it firms, but only as needed.

2. Take one spoonful of the mixture at a time and roll it between the palms of your hands into a ball shape. Flatten the ball between the palms of your hands into a round cookie shape about 2 inches in diameter.

(continued on next page)

3. Remove the cookie sheet from the freezer. Place the flattened peanut butter balls on top of the cookie layer side by side and leaving a little space in between each one. Return the cookie sheet to the freezer for approximately 15 minutes to firm.

Assembly (part 1):

1. Remove the cookie sheet from the freezer. Using the tip of a knife, cut around each flattened peanut butter ball, like you would a cookie cutter, so the cookie layers are the same size as the flattened peanut butter balls. When finished, you should have ten two-layer cookies (peanut butter layer on top of a cookie layer). Remove the excess cookie mixture from the cookie sheet. Set aside.

Prepare the chocolate coating:

1. Add all ingredients for the chocolate coating to a small saucepan and melt on lowest heat until it's completely melted and smooth, taking care to not let it burn.

2. Dip each two-layer cookie into the chocolate coating so the cookie is completely covered on all sides; use a fork to flip them over and to let the excess chocolate drip off.

Assembly (part 2):

1. Place the cookies back onto the cookie sheet. Return the cookie sheet to the freezer for approximately 30 minutes, or until the chocolate hardens.

2. Store in an air-tight container in the freezer or refrigerator until ready to serve, because they will get soft if left out at room temperature.

CHOCOLATE TRIPLE NUT CLUSTERS

Yields: 12 pieces | **Prep Time:** 10 minutes | **Inactive Time:** 60 minutes

INGREDIENTS

½ cup walnuts
½ cup pecans
½ cup peanuts
½ cup peanut butter
½ cup maple syrup
¼ cup cacao powder
2 tablespoons coconut oil
½ teaspoon vanilla extract

DIRECTIONS

1. Prepare a cookie sheet lined with parchment paper. Set aside.

2. Break the walnuts, pecans, and peanuts into small pieces by hand, or add them to a food processor and pulse 8 to 10 times until they are broken down into small pieces, taking care to not over process.

3. Add all ingredients, including the chopped nuts, to a medium-sized bowl and stir until everything is well combined and smooth.

4. Take one spoonful of the mixture at a time and drop it onto the prepared cookie sheet.

5. Place the cookie sheet in the freezer for approximately 60 minutes, or until the chocolate hardens.

6. Store in an air-tight container in the freezer until ready to serve, because they will get soft if left out at room temperature.

PECAN PRALINES

Yields: 10 pieces | **Prep Time:** 10 minutes | **Inactive Time:** 60 minutes

INGREDIENTS

For the pralines:
1 cup medjool dates, pitted
2 tablespoons almond butter
1 tablespoon coconut oil
¼ teaspoon vanilla extract
¼ teaspoon sea salt

For the add-in:
1 cup pecans

DIRECTIONS

1. Prepare a cookie sheet lined with parchment paper. Set aside.

2. Add all ingredients for the pralines to a food processor and process until the dates are broken down into small pieces and everything is well combined, taking care to not over process.

3. Add the pecan add-in to the food processor and stir in by hand until they are evenly distributed.

4. Take one spoonful at a time and drop it onto the prepared cookie sheet.

5. Transfer the cookie sheet to the freezer for approximately 60 minutes, or until the pralines are firm.

6. Store in an air-tight container in the freezer until they are ready to serve, because the pralines will get soft if left out at room temperature.

DARK CHOCOLATE PISTACHIO FUDGE

Yields: 8 small squares | **Prep Time:** 10 minutes | **Inactive Time:** 60 minutes

INGREDIENTS

For the chocolate fudge:
½ cup cacao powder
¼ cup coconut oil
¼ cup maple syrup
¼ cup almond butter
1 teaspoon vanilla extract

For the add-in:
½ cup pistachios

For the pistachio garnish:
¼ cup pistachios, chopped

DIRECTIONS

Prepare the chocolate fudge:

1. Prepare a 9 × 5 loaf pan lined with parchment paper. Set aside.

2. Add all ingredients for the chocolate fudge to a medium-sized bowl and stir until everything is well combined and smooth.

3. Add the pistachio add-in and stir in by hand until they are evenly distributed.

4. Transfer the mixture into the prepared loaf pan and spread it evenly on the bottom of the pan.

Assembly:

1. Sprinkle the pistachio garnish evenly over the top of the chocolate fudge and gently pat it down so it's slightly embedded into the chocolate fudge.

2. Place the loaf pan in the freezer for approximately 60 minutes, or until the fudge is firm.

3. Remove the loaf pan from the freezer and cut into 8 small squares.

4. Store in an air-tight container in the freezer or refrigerator until ready to serve, because the fudge will get soft if left out at room temperature.

RASPBERRY MACAROONS

Yields: 8 pieces | **Prep Time:** 10 minutes | **Inactive Time:** 60 minutes

INGREDIENTS

For the macaroons:
1¼ cups unsweetened shredded coconut
1 cup freeze-dried raspberries
¼ cup almond flour
¼ cup maple syrup
3 tablespoons coconut oil
⅛ teaspoon sea salt

For the chocolate drizzle:
½ cup semi-sweet mini chocolate chips
1 teaspoon coconut oil

DIRECTIONS

Prepare the macaroons:

1. Prepare a cookie sheet lined with parchment paper. Set aside.

2. Add all ingredients for the macaroons to a food processor and process until everything is well combined.

3. Using a 1½-inch cookie scoop or a regular spoon, take one scoop of the mixture at a time and drop it onto the prepared cookie sheet. If using a spoon, use your fingertips to shape it into a round mound shape.

4. Transfer the cookie sheet to the freezer for approximately 30 minutes, or until the macaroons firm.

Prepare the chocolate drizzle:

1. Add all ingredients for the chocolate drizzle to a small saucepan and melt on lowest heat, stirring until it is completely melted and smooth, taking care to not let it burn.

Assembly:

1. Remove the cookie sheet from the freezer. Take each macaroon and dip the bottom one-quarter of it into the melted chocolate and place it back onto the cookie sheet.

2. Using a spoon, drizzle the remaining melted chocolate over the top of each macaroon.

3. Return the cookie sheet to the freezer for approximately 30 minutes, or until the chocolate hardens.

4. Store in an air-tight container in the freezer or refrigerator until ready to serve, because the macaroons will get soft if left out at room temperature.

About the Author

Karielyn Tillman is the creator of the website *The Healthy Family and Home*, where she shares easy, clean eating, vegan, and gluten-free recipes made with nutrient-dense, real food ingredients. Her area of expertise is making healthier versions of traditional recipes that are made with highly processed ingredients. She is passionate about teaching others to read food labels and how to make clean recipes with healthier ingredients.

Her recipes have been featured on more than 250 websites, including *Redbook*, *Country Living*, *Boston Magazine*, *ELLE*, *Dr. Axe*, *Kris Carr*, Yahoo!, MSN, *One Green Planet*, *Brit + Co*, *Epicurious*, *Food52*, *Delish*, *BuzzFeed*, and many more. Karielyn's recipes and photos have been published in *Go Gluten Free!* magazine, *Gluten-Free Living* magazine, and *The Non-GMO Cookbook: Recipes and Advice for a Non-GMO Lifestyle*, as well as in several digital publications, iPhone recipe apps, and digital cookbook collaborations.

As a recipe developer, she's created recipes for brands such as Vibrant Health, Naturally More, Rawmio Gourmet Chocolate Spreads, Sambazon, Sunwarrior, Natera, and more. She has worked with national brands like Whole Foods, Maty's Healthy Products, and ALOHA to create brand awareness for their products.

Karielyn lives near New Orleans, Louisiana, with her husband and two young sons, and she enjoys traveling with her family.

Conversion Chart

METRIC AND IMPERIAL CONVERSIONS
(These conversions are rounded for convenience)

Ingredient	Cups/Tablespoons/Teaspoons	Ounces	Grams/Milliliters
Coconut butter	1 cup/16 tablespoons	8 ounces	230 grams
Flour, almond	1 cup/1 tablespoon	4.5 ounces/0.3 ounce	125 grams/8 grams
Flour, coconut	1 cup	4 ounces	120 grams
Fruit, dried	1 cup	4 ounces	120 grams
Fruits, chopped	1 cup	5 to 7 ounces	145 to 200 grams
Fruits, puréed	1 cup	8.5 ounces	245 grams
Maple syrup	1 tablespoon	0.75 ounce	20 grams
Liquids: water or juice	1 cup	8 fluid ounces	240 milliliters
Oats	1 cup	5.5 ounces	150 grams
Salt	1 teaspoon	0.2 ounces	6 grams
Spices: cinnamon, cloves, ginger (ground), pumpkin spice	1 teaspoon	0.2 ounce	5 milliliters
Sugar, coconut, firmly packed	1 cup	7 ounces	200 grams
Vanilla extract	1 teaspoon	0.2 ounce	4 grams

Index